A Cartoon History
of
Roosevelt's Career

Theodore Roosevelt in 1904

This portrait, taken in the year of Mr. Roosevelt's election to the Presidency of the United States,
is one of his best photographs

A Cartoon History

of

Roosevelt's Career

Illustrated by Six Hundred and Thirty Contemporary

Cartoons and Many Other Pictures

By Albert Shaw

New York:

The Review of Reviews Company

Publishers

PREFACE

——————

IT has long been my custom to make note of political cartoons and caricatures in the press of various countries. It requires, perhaps, some understanding of political questions and personages, and some acquaintance with the types and symbols used in caricature, to appreciate altogether the meaning and value of that kind of work. But when one has acquired a certain amount of knowledge and familiarity in this field, he is sure to find the current cartoons very enlightening as well as amusing. The cartoonists, indeed, reflect more faithfully the changing phases of the public mind than do the writers of editorial articles.

The political writer must exercise a certain dignity and restraint. But the cartoonist is a privileged character, who may tell the plain, homely truth as people see it and feel it, very much as the court jester in olden times was expected to take liberties with those in high places and—under the guise of quip and fling and witticism—tell the king a bit of direct and wholesome truth. Thus I have not hesitated to make constant use, in reproduced form, of American and foreign cartoons from month to month in the *Review of Reviews*, not merely because they are diverting, but chiefly because they frequently express so much of fact and sentiment and point of view, in such telling and convincing ways.

For a long time there were mechanical difficulties in the way of the large use of illustration in daily newspapers. Pictorial matter of all kinds was chiefly confined to the weekly and monthly illustrated publications. The large and influential use of cartoons was, therefore, confined to a set of weekly periodicals, not very numerous, that made a specialty of political subjects. Of all these, it is needless to say the most famous has been *Punch*, of London. In this country *Harper's* and *Leslie's* weeklies, followed by *Puck* and *Judge*, have been the most famous and influential of the weekly papers making use of cartoons in such a manner as to express and influence political opinion throughout the country.

In all the European countries, political cartoons have for many years been used with great effect. In Germany the publishers of papers using cartoons have at times been subjected to a rather severe censorship; but in the main throughout Europe there is permitted an extreme freedom of expression to cartoonists that would not be tolerated in political writers. And there is a fierceness of satire, and a malignancy of attack, in many of these European cartoons that would not accord with the kindlier and more humorous tone of American cartoon work.

The very rapid growth, during recent years, of the use of cartoons in the daily newspapers of the United States has been due to the improvement of photo-engraving methods which permit the very rapid making of a zinc-etched block in reproduction of a pen drawing. Thus the cartoon as drawn this afternoon in illustration of the latest political incident, may be as readily printed in to-morrow morning's paper as the letter-press itself that reports the news. There are few people who realize the extent to which inventions of this kind are changing the methods and character of the press.

It is hardly less remarkable, however, that the use of photo-engraving in newspaper offices should have been followed so quickly by the development of a great number of clever American cartoonists. It had seemed at one time that John Tenniel, afterwards knighted in recognition of the importance of his cartoon work in *Punch*, could have no successor worthy of the name. But *Punch* keeps its hold, and England has several very clever political cartoonists at this moment. And it had seemed at one time that the political cartoon could have no future in America, after Nast and his two or three contemporaries. But then came the school of Keppler and Gillam, whose marvelous work, printed in colors by lithography, made *Puck* a power in the land, interpreting—perhaps better than any other newspaper or periodical—the aims and achievements of President Cleveland. It was cartoonists of this same school and method who, with similar ability, represented the Republican point of view in the weekly paper called *Judge*.

Then came the rise to influence and power of the cartoonists of the daily press, the foremost of these being the late Charles G. Bush, for several years on the New York *Herald* and then for many years on the New York *World*. One is tempted to run over the list of remarkable men who within the past fifteen or twenty years have been drawing cartoons for the American newspapers and periodicals. But this volume—which is chiefly theirs rather than mine—shows well enough my estimate of their wit, their humor, their kindliness, and, above all, their remarkable instinct for politics.

Their drawing has had to be done under great pressure; and some of the most influential and effective of them all are quite defective when judged from the standpoint of draughtsmanship. But where their drawing is often greatly at fault when compared, for example, with such a piece of work as that of Bernard Partridge of *Punch* on page 75 of this volume, their cartoons have been redeemed by the skill with which they expressed their ideas. The artists of *Punch*, drawing perhaps only one finished cartoon a week, have a much better opportunity to do good technical work than the newspaper cartoonists who often draw an effective cartoon each day for weeks together.

Of all the political personages who have become familiar in cartoons, no one in recent years has figured as frequently as Mr. Roosevelt. And we have no other public man whose career has been illustrated in contemporary cartoons so continuously, or for such a long time. Mr. Nast's cartoons were drawn on the blocks which were laboriously tooled by the wood-engravers. He did not waste much effort on minor personages. And Mr. Nast's tributes to Roosevelt give fine testimony to the impression the young reformer in the New York Legislature was making upon public opinion in State and nation.

As our readers will discover, we have been able to find striking cartoons that bear witness, in each successive phase of Roosevelt's career, to the recognition accorded him at the moment as a man of energy and leadership who was taking hold of essential problems rather than giving his energy to lesser things. I believe, therefore, that these cartoons, brought together in such a way as to bear upon successive episodes or periods in Mr. Roosevelt's public life, will be found useful as a contribution to the political history of our own time.

Very much of the material assembled here is of a nature so ephemeral that its assembling has not been a very easy task. For example, although the *Verdict* ran its brief but brilliant career of two or three years as recently as 1899-1900, my own office file had disappeared, and it was not easy to obtain access to the copies in which Roosevelt as Governor and Vice-Presidential nominee was so strikingly presented, until Mr. Alfred Henry Lewis, who had been its editor, generously lent his own personal file. Thus thanks are also due to the Columbia College Library, the Astor Library, and to the editors and proprietors of *Puck*, of *Judge*, of *Harper's Weekly*, of *Leslie's*, of *Collier's*, and of several other periodicals. I am much indebted also to several members of my own office staff for toilsome search in the files of newspapers.

Recognition is due in this place to Mr. William Menkel, of the editorial office of the *Review of Reviews*, more than to any one else, for co-operation without which the assembling and arrangement of so much pictorial matter would have been very laborious and difficult. There is such a thing as making one cartoon add to the effectiveness of another by the manner of their grouping on the same page. This is also true of the contrasts or the cumulative impressions produced in arrangement of facing pages. To Mr. Menkel I am much indebted for help in all this,—which, if it may seem easy in the result, was more difficult than anything else in the actual doing.

I have tried to make the simple text of this volume a clear and honest interpretation of what Mr. Roosevelt has tried to do as a public man, and the spirit he has shown throughout his career. I have had some advantages of intimate knowledge of most of the period I present in these cursory pages; and this has included acquaintance not only with the hero of the play but with most of the other people who have been prominently associated with him upon our political stage. I hope, therefore, that the collection of cartoons and other pictures, with the thread of text that binds them together, may find some modest place with the materials that a historian like Mr. James Ford Rhodes, for example, would some day like to use as helping him to throw into true historical perspective the political period in which Mr. Roosevelt has been so notable and dominant a figure.

ALBERT SHAW.

NEW YORK, *August 22,* 1910.

CONTENTS

A Cartoon History
of Roosevelt's Career

CHAPTER I

His First Political Experiences

IT so happened that Theodore Roosevelt became a national figure at the very beginning of his public career. His name was printed in newspapers from one ocean to the other, his portrait duly appeared in the illustrated press, and he was conspicuous enough to be caricatured by political cartoonists in the days when it was not customary for the wood engravers to carve the lineaments of any except those who, for good or for ill, were among the eminent personages of the hour.

There might be some difference of opinion about the quality of Mr. Roosevelt's mental endowments; but there could never be any difference about his courage, his single-heartedness, his concentration upon the thing in hand, and the clear, strong, stubborn will power to do his best under any given circumstances, and to see in any piece of work, whether public or private, quite sufficient opportunity to justify his best endeavor.

Doubtless some conditions, not of his own choosing or making, have aided Mr. Roosevelt in the successive onward steps of his public career. But when one studies the case thoroughly, one must admit that Mr. Roosevelt has made his own way by his own efforts, just as truly as did Mr. Lincoln, or any other man of distinction in our history. The city boy, brought up in affluent circumstances, who scorns ease, deliberately chooses a life of work and of usefulness, and never for a moment doubts the value of his ideals, deserves just as much credit as the country boy who pores over his few treasured books by the dim evening light in his log cabin.

Thus far in our history it has not made very much difference. Most American boys have had a fairly good chance to improve their own positions, and to be of use to their fellow men, if only they were endowed with will, energy, some gift of moral power, and some little kindling touch of imagination.

As a boy, Theodore Roosevelt was rather sickly than strong, and he gave few signs pointing to a very exceptional future. But he was plucky and persevering. He became strong by degrees through physical exercise, and through a gradual acquirement of the art of living in such a way as to be hardy and well. He graduated at Harvard in 1880, and was twenty-two years old October 27 of that year, having been born in 1858.

His father, also named Theodore Roosevelt, was a man of business and affairs in New York City. He was prominent in all that made for the best interests of New York, noted for philanthropic works, sound in his principles, wise and devoted as a father. He died a year or two before his son and namesake finished the Harvard course. The family had lived in and about New York City for more than two hundred and fifty years.

During the college period, Theodore Roosevelt was a diligent student, devoting himself especially to out-door science, American history, and literary studies. He was active in almost every form of exercise and sport, and took creditable rank in everything, although he was never a champion athlete. He learned to ride well, and played polo. He learned to shoot, and made the most of his vacations. He was fond of animal life and nature, and cultivated that habit of close observation which has made him a naturalist and has added so much to his happiness in life. He took to the water, with Long Island Sound offering ready access; and his appetite for the study of American naval history was whetted by some practical knowledge of boats and seamanship.

Thus, soon after leaving college, he wrote and published his first book, on the " Naval War of 1812 "; and the greatness of the American navy to-day is largely due to such experiences and studies as produced that excellent volume. After leaving college, Mr. Roosevelt spent about a year in further study and foreign travel. It was characteristic of him that in that year he did some difficult mountain climbing and qualified himself for membership in the famous Alpine Club of London, his sponsors being Mr. Bryce and Mr. Buxton, whose careers have been so distinguished and useful, and who have been Mr. Roosevelt's life-long friends.

His year of travel and study ended, Mr. Roosevelt settled down in his native city, determined to be a good citizen and to do with his might whatsoever his hand found to do. In his private capacity, he was reading law, with a view to taking up a profession that he has never yet found an opportunity to practise. He was also studying American history and beginning to write his books.

On the public side of his life, he was trying to find out how we were really governed in the city and State of New York. He proposed to take a citizen's part in the governing business, and he set out to acquaint himself with the practical as well as the theoretical mechanism of politics and government. He soon discovered that he must join a political organization, attend the primaries, and do his part at the local political headquarters.

He studied his own voting precinct, his municipal ward, and his assembly district. He found himself a Republican by inheritance and tradition, and by his own study of the course of the country's political history. He attached himself, therefore, to the Republican organization of his district, and insisted upon taking his place as an active worker.

He was not taken seriously at first by the workers and heelers in the old Jake

THEODORE ROOSEVELT

(As a student at Harvard)

"EXCELSIOR!" (the motto of New York State.)
(A later cartoon emblematic of Mr. Roosevelt's career.)
From the *Inquirer* (Philadelphia)

Hess district; but it was not many weeks before his positive and serious qualities were apparent to everybody. There was dissatisfaction with the district's leadership, and with its member of the legislature. Young Roosevelt was ready for the fight, secured the nomination, and was elected a member of the law-making body of the State.

This was in the fall of 1881; and he served in the legislature during the sessions of 1882, 1883, and 1884.

There were in the United States several thousand members of State legislatures at that time, many of whom must have had ability, and not a few of whom were laying foundations for future eminence. But among all those thousands, young Roosevelt at that time took positions which gave him an immediate recognition throughout the country. He had a way of finding what were the great issues and driving straight at them, with no thought of waiting for more experience, or of deferring to older men. It was not vanity or egotism that impelled him, but earnestness and his great, life-long talent for decision and action.

He was, of course, fortunate in the stage that was set for the part he had to play. New York State was the foremost of our commonwealths, and New York City was our chief metropolis. Reforms in the administration of his State and city were sure to be noted throughout the land.

He saw dawning upon the horizon of practical politics two essential reforms. One was the movement to substitute for the old spoils system in nation, State and city, a business-like civil service, based upon merit and efficiency regardless of party. The other was the improvement of the methods and character of our municipal government, in view of the rapid growth of town life. He studied the civil-service question, and identified himself with the national and State civil-service reform associations.

THEODORE ROOSEVELT
(From a photograph taken while a member of the
New York Legislature.)

The Hon. Carl Schurz, serving as Secretary of the Interior from 1877 to 1881, was promoting the movement at Washington; George William Curtis was at its head in New York; leading Massachusetts men were identified with it, and Theodore Roosevelt at once took his place with these men. He wrote the civil-service law for the State of New York, and secured its passage. This was a great achievement, because the spoils system was firmly intrenched.

He secured a legislative investigation of New York City government, and headed the committee of inquiry. He secured the passage of a law increasing the authority of the mayor, and in various other ways improved the city charter, while reforming abuses in many offices.

Grover Cleveland, who had been a reform mayor of the city of Buffalo, was elected governor in 1882, and although he was a Democrat, while Roosevelt was a Republican, there was co-operation between the two men in the work of purifying politics and administration in the State and its cities and counties. The position that young Roosevelt then occupied in the public eye is admirably shown in a cartoon drawn by Nast in the spring of 1884, in which Governor Cleveland and Theodore Roosevelt are represented as working out reforms for New York that would prevent such disorder and bloodshed as had at that time occurred in the city of Cincinnati. It is a felicitous thing that this first important cartoon in which the face of Roosevelt appears should associate him with Mr. Cleveland. Each man was destined to become President of the United States. They were friends to the day of Mr. Cleveland's death.

So vigorous was Mr. Roosevelt's work in the legislatures of 1882 and 1883, that he was prominently mentioned for the Speakership of the Assembly that convened in January, 1884. His work in that session was so noteworthy that it made him famous throughout the country, and he would have remained a prominent and respected leader in public affairs even if he had never held another office.

THE SEAL OF THE STATE OF NEW YORK
From the *World* (New York, 1906)

REFORM WITHOUT BLOODSHED

(Governor Cleveland and Theodore Roosevelt at their good work.)

From *Harper's Weekly*, April 19, 1884

OUR NEW WATCHMAN—ROOSEVELT
(Our political boss and henchman must go.)
From *Harper's Weekly*, May 10, 1884

Young men of like views and aspirations in other States all the way to the Pacific took note of this courageous young leader in New York, and felt that they might some day bring him forward as their candidate for the Presidency. His Dakota ranch and his studies of Western history and pioneer life were already becoming a factor in his larger reputation. What proved to be the turning point in his political career lay just ahead of him, although it could not be clearly foreseen.

CHAPTER II

The Crisis of 1884

MR. ROOSEVELT was made one of the four delegates-at-large from New York to the national Republican convention of 1884, and was chosen as chairman of the State delegation. This was a very unusual honor for so young a man, and is an evidence of the influential rank he had already attained. James A. Garfield had been elected President in 1880, but his assassination had placed the Vice-President, Mr. Arthur, of New York, in the White House. The idol of the Republican masses of the Middle West was the Speaker of the House, Mr. James G. Blaine, of Maine. President Arthur was a candidate for renomination, and many of the anti-Blaine men rallied about him. He belonged to the "Stalwart" faction of the party in New York, of which Senator Conkling was the mentor, while Mr. Blaine was the inspiration of the so-called "Half-breeds" of the Empire State.

Roosevelt was not in alliance with either faction; and he strongly hoped, with many of the reformers and conservative men of the day, that it might be possible to secure the nomination as a compromise candidate of Senator Edmunds, of Vermont, then the strongest and most respected figure in the United States Senate.

Popular sentiment triumphed, and Mr. Blaine was nominated. The reformers admitted Mr. Blaine's brilliancy as a party leader, but distrusted his judgment and his character. Until that time, Carl Schurz, George William Curtis, Henry Ward Beecher, and many other prominent reformers had been acknowledged leaders of the Republican party. Curtis and Schurz had been great figures in Republican conventions. They were deeply disaffected by the nomination of Blaine and went home in silence, waiting to see what the Democrats would do. Mr. Roosevelt, meanwhile, went out to his Dakota ranch, primarily to attend to his cattle business, but also to think over the political situation.

The Democrats had the wisdom to nominate Governor Cleveland, of New York, and the disaffected Republicans, led by Schurz and Curtis, organized the so-called "Independent" or "Mugwump" movement, and decided to support Cleveland against Blaine.

THE NEW VOYAGE BEGUN
(An emblematic cartoon of a later period)
From the *North American* (Philadelphia)

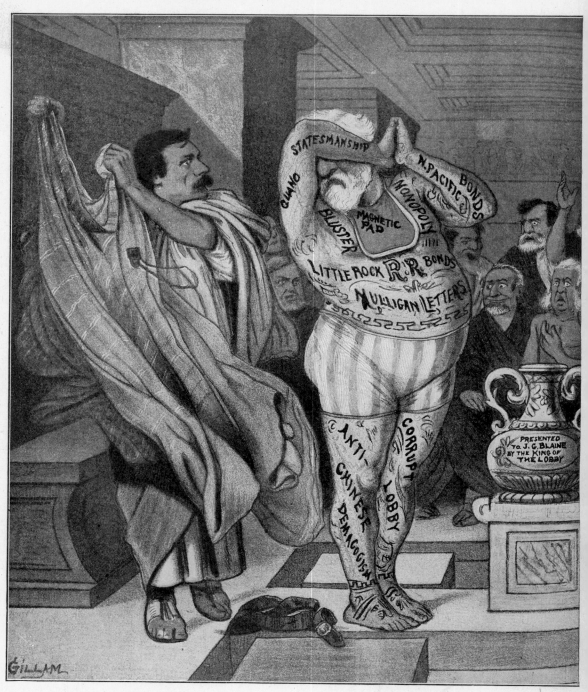

PHRYNE BEFORE THE CHICAGO

ARDENT ADVOCATE: " Now, gentlemen, don't make any mistake in

Mr. Whitelaw Reid, of the New York *Tribune*, is presenting James G. Blaine to the Republican convention of 1884
figure from the reader's right. On Mr. Roosevelt's left, in their order, appear Carl Schurz, Senator Evarts,
next to Sherman is John A. Logan, with his black hair and heavy mustache. Other notable delegates are

TRIBUNAL.—From *Puck*, June 4, 1884.

your decision. Here's Purity and Magnetism for you. Can't be beat!"

t Chicago. Mr. Roosevelt, as chairman of the powerful New York delegation, is seen in the front row, the fourth
nd George William Curtis.   Immediately behind Mr. Roosevelt is John Sherman, with the white hair, while
scattered about in the group.

LITTLE BO-PEEP, LOST HER SHEEP,
AND DIDN'T KNOW WHERE TO FIND THEM;

(The "lost sheep" in this cartoon are those Republicans who vigorously opposed Mr. Blaine at the Chicago conv
of Vermont. After the convention had given its voice for the "Plumed Knight," however, Mr. Roosevelt, instead
lican fold and gave his entire support to the party throughout the campaign. See Mr. Roosevelt's statement on th

From *Judge*, June 21, 1884

OH! LET THEM ALONE, AND THEY'LL COME HOME,
AND CARRY THEIR TAILS BEHIND THEM.

tion of 1884. Prominent among these was Mr. Roosevelt, whose candidate for the nomination was Senator Edmunds, bolting the party and joining in the independent movement with Schurz, Curtis, and others, remained in the Repub- subject on page 12.)

THE SIZE OF THE INDEPENDENT ARMY

This is the third time they have marched around. There are just about nine of them, not ninety thousand.
(It was mistakenly assumed that Roosevelt would join in the movement.)—From *Judge*, July, 1884.

It was believed by the Independents and the Democrats that Roosevelt would also
support Cleveland; and even the Blaine Republicans had little hope of holding him within party lines. But after a b.. f interval, Mr. Roosevelt came out with a public statement so characteristic of him t.. it ought to be quoted in this record. It was as follows:

"I intend to vote the Republican P.. 'ential ticket. A man cannot act both without and within the
party; he can do either, but he cannot pos.. do both. Each course has its advantages, and each has its
disadvantages, and one cannot take the advan.. or the disadvantages separately. I went in with my eyes
open to do what I could within the party; I d.. ·y best and got beaten, and I propose to stand by the result. It is impossible to combine the functions o.. guerrilla chief with those of a colonel in the regular
army; one has greater independence of action, the ot.. r is able to make what action he does take vastly
more effective. In certain contingencies, the one can do the most good; in certain contingencies, the other;
but there is no use in accepting a commission and then trying to play the game out on a lone hand. During
the entire canvass for the nomination Mr. Blaine received but two checks. I had a hand in both, and I
could have had a hand in neither had not those Republicans who elected me the head of the New York
State delegation supposed that I would in good· faith support the man who was fairly made the Republican nominee. I am, by inheritance and by education, a Republican; whatever good I have been able to
accomplish in public life has been accomplished through the ·Republican party; I have acted with it in the
past, and wish to act with it in the future."

The cartoons relating to this period that are reproduced herewith indicate how general was the belief that Mr. Roosevelt would abandon his party. Grover Cleveland was his personal friend; and his views were regarded as more nearly like Roosevelt's than were those of the successful Republican candidate. But Roosevelt believed that his place was with the Republican party, and that in the long run he could be far more useful to the country as a member of his own political organization than as a critical outsider.

Bereavements in his family just at this time lessened his public activity; but he made some speeches before the campaign was over, and indulged in no bitterness toward those who reproached him for abandoning the leadership of Curtis and Schurz. He had predicted,—while the fight was on in the convention and there was some chance to nominate Edmunds,—that Blaine could not be elected. The issue in November was very close; but the Democrats won and Grover Cleveland was inaugurated as President in March, 1885.

Mr. Roosevelt had maintained the party regularity that was a valuable asset in his subsequent political career, while by his position in the convention of 1884 and during the campaign he had firmly established his position as a man of independence and self-direction within the party councils. He followed no political boss in the New York organization, and he worshipped at the shrine of no popular idol. He was never wholly forgiven by Mr. Schurz and the leaders of the revolt; nor, on the other hand, was he ever in full favor with Mr. Blaine and those closest to the ambitions of the so-called "Plumed Knight."

But he had worked out a consistent line of action for himself, and on more than one occasion in subsequent years, when there might have seemed some good reason of the moment for acting in opposition, he preferred to stay in the Republican camp, while freely criticising the party's mistakes.

THE COWBOY AND THE LOCOMOTIVE (*See next chapter.*)

A very simple little story of the political plains, plainly told. (Roosevelt, as the Republican "cowboy" candidate for Mayor of New York, trying to lasso the Democracy, with Abram Hewitt at its head.)

From the *World* (New York), October 31, 1886

CHAPTER III

The Mayoralty Fight of 1886

MR. ROOSEVELT had bought his ranch in the "Bad Lands" of Northwest Dakota near the Montana line on the Little Missouri River in the summer of 1883, and had invested a good deal of his patrimony in the cattle business. He had returned to his ranch after the convention of 1884, and was much absorbed in all the phases of frontier life, remaining almost continuously for the following two years. He had published a book on various hunting experiences in 1883. He founded the Boone and Crockett Club, and sought to know by experience as well as by study all those phases of pioneer life that had made the American people what they are.

Yet he had by no means severed the ties that bound him to New York. Like the Roosevelts before him, he had grown up at once a townsman of Manhattan and a country-man of Long Island. It would not have been like him to transplant himself altogether. He could identify himself with the Dakota pion-eer experiences, but it would not have been in keeping with his nature to break the con-tinuity of the Roosevelt life in and about the great town that had grown up where the original Roosevelts had settled.

Even while he was writing his books on ranch life and the pursuit of large game in the Rockies, and while at work on his chief historical production, "The Winning of the West," he also produced a history of the City of New York which was published in 1890. He had spent some part of each winter in New York City; and when the municipal re-formers brought him out as their candidate for mayor in 1886 he could not refuse.

The Republican party promptly made him its candidate. His father had been mayor be-fore him, and he himself while in the leg-islature had only recently secured charter changes for the metropolis and given great attention to its affairs. Mr. Henry George,

MR. ROOSEVELT
(In hunting costume of the early '80s.)

THE MAYORALTY CONTEST—THEY HAD THEIR LITTLE BOOMS
From the New York *World*, October 17, 1886

who was then at the height of his fame, had come from San Francisco to live in New York; and the labor party, together with the believers in Mr. George's single-tax theory, made him a candidate for the chief city office. Tammany Hall and the Democratic party nominated an able business man and member of Congress, Mr. Abram S. Hewitt, son-in-law of Peter Cooper.

It was a stirring campaign. As election day approached, certain conservative business interests were alarmed lest Henry George should win, and to make sure of his defeat they decided to vote with the Democrats for Mr. Hewitt. The alarm about Mr. George is well expressed in a cartoon from *Harper's Weekly* that we reproduce. Mr. Roosevelt received more than 60,000 votes; Mr. George more than 68,000, and Mr. Hewitt more

THE RIVAL GUIDES

(Roosevelt, Hewitt, and Henry George as mayoralty candidates.)

A Worthy Old Gentleman of Manhattan City (Father Knickerbocker), accustomed to take to the woods every other November, was accosted by two experienced guides, each bent on taking him a different path. They were so enthusiastic over their routes that while belaboring one another with arguments, an Incompetent Guide (Henry George) sprang from the brush, and seizing the old gentleman by the throat, attempted to drag him into a very dangerous by-way much frequented by lawless men, when——

MORAL.—There can be no moral to this until the Freebooter is taken from the scene.

From *Harper's Weekly*, October 30, 1886

than 90,000. New York at that time was a strong Democratic city, and Mr. Roosevelt's vote, under all the circumstances, was highly creditable.

His defeat was not a disappointment. He had sprung unexpectedly into the forefront of political life within a year or two after leaving college, and he needed an interval of private life for further reading and study, the building up of his mental and physical constitution, and the ordering of his personal and private affairs.

CHAPTER IV
A Brief Period of Private Life

THE Western life that Mr. Roosevelt led in the eighties is not likely to be overestimated by any biographer as a formative influence in shaping his mature character, and as relating itself in many ways to his later career as leader of the nation. Its human contacts were direct, unconventional, and sincere. Mr. Roosevelt became hardy by long days in the saddle and the pursuit of game in the fastnesses of the mountains. His graduating theme at Harvard had been in the field of natural history; and the Western life made him a high authority upon the animals of the North American continent.

He found time in this period to read standard literature and become saturated with it; and he became firmly grounded in the habit of giving literary expression to his own observations and experiences. The years 1887 and 1888 were devoted to this Western life, to historical study and writing, and to domestic life and the founding of a home and family.

The Roosevelt kith and kin had long been identified with the Oyster Bay neighborhood of Long Island, and it was natural and easy for Theodore Roosevelt to settle there and to build on the

THEODORE ROOSEVELT AS HE LOOKED IN RANCHING DAYS

MR. ROOSEVELT'S ELKHORN RANCH BUILDINGS
(From a sketch by Remington, courtesy of Century Co.)

top of his Sagamore Hill the modest but ample and comfortable home that has since become so famous, and that is pictured (as it then looked) at the end of this chapter.

Some years ago, at the request of the writer of the

MR. ROOSEVELT'S RANCH ON THE LITTLE MISSOURI, IN THE BAD LANDS

A SUCCESSFUL HUNTING TRIP (MR. ROOSEVELT ON THE RIGHT)

present volume, the late Julian Ralph prepared an admirable character sketch of Theodore Roosevelt. Much of it is in the form of direct statement by Mr. Roosevelt himself. One of the paragraphs sums up, in his own words, Roosevelt's period of life in Dakota. "A man with a horse and a gun is a picture or idea that has always appealed to me," he says. "Mayne Reid's heroes and the life out West also always appealed to me. I wanted to see the rude, rough, formative life in the Far West before it vanished. I went there just in time. I was in at the killing of the buffalo, in the last big hunt, in 1883, near Pretty Buttes, when the whites and the Sioux from Standing Rock and Pine Ridge were doing the killing. I went West while I was in the Assembly, in the long vacations—went hunting—went to the Bad Lands and shot elk, sheep, deer, buffalo, and antelope. I made two hunting trips, and in 1884 I started my cattle ranch. After my terms in the Legislature, and until I was appointed Civil Service Commissioner, I lived most of the time out West in the summers and spent only the winters in New York. I

YOU MAY MAKE THE HORSE NERVOUS, BOYS, BUT YOU CAN'T UNSEAT THE RIDER

(A typical later cartoon, based upon Mr. Roosevelt's Western life, as a favorite theme.—*Judge*)

never was happier in my life. My house out there is a long low house of hewn logs, which I helped to build myself. It has a broad veranda and rocking chairs and a big fireplace and elk skins and wolf skins scattered about,—on the brink of the Little Missouri, right in a clump of cotton woods; and less than three years ago I shot a deer from the veranda. I kept my books there,—such as I wanted, —and did a deal of writing, being the rest of the time out all day in every kind of weather."

These sentences, taken together with the pictures with which this brief chapter of our volume is embellished, enable one to understand quite clearly how it came about that the ranching period of his life entered into the very structure of Roosevelt's character and mind. And they also explain why in after years his frequent hunting trips were indispensable. The later quest of great game in Africa was in response to that persistent call of outdoor life, and love of wilderness adventure, that has always belonged to Mr. Roosevelt's essential nature.

ROOSEVELT AS A "BRONCHO BUSTER"

A SHOT BY MR. ROOSEVELT FROM THE VERANDA OF HIS RANCH HOUSE
From Roosevelt's Wilderness Hunter, copyright 1893 by G. P. Putnams Sons.

ONE OF MR. ROOSEVELT'S QUIET DAYS

(Three cartoons in this page are from drawings by John T. McCutcheon for the Chicago *Tribune*. They are of a much later period, but are all illustrative of Roosevelt as a hunter in the Northwestern wilderness. See also next page.)

"HURRY UP, BOYS, I'VE GOT 'EM TREED!"

"THE PRESIDENT HAS BEEN ON THE TRAIL OF A GRIZZLY FOR FOUR DAYS.—[News item.]

THE REAL BRONCHO BUSTER
Teddy Roosevelt seems to stick pretty tight to his political mount.
(Another later cartoon based on a favorite theme.)
From the *Journal* (Minneapolis)

I WISH THE BOYS'D GET UP.   HERE I'VE HAD
BREAKFAST READY AN HOUR

"COME ON, BOYS!   I'VE GOT 'EM CORNERED"

(These two cartoons belong to the series from which reproductions are made on the previous page.   Mr. McCutch-eon drew them for the Chicago *Tribune* when Mr. Roosevelt was taking a Presidential vacation in the Northwest country.   Few cartoonists have understood Roosevelt in all his phases as well as Mr. McCutcheon, who has given us some of his best examples in a book called "T. R. in Cartoons," published by Messrs. A. C. McClurg & Co., of Chicago.)

MR. ROOSEVELT'S HOUSE AT OYSTER BAY (NEW YORK) AS ORIGINALLY BUILT BY HIM

THE BRAVE LITTLE GIANT-KILLER

Spoils-System Giant: "Calm yourself, Theodore. If you go too far, you'll find yourself jerked back mighty sudden by President Harrison!"

From *Puck*. Copyright, 1889. By permission

CHAPTER V

Battling with the Spoils System

IN the campaign of 1888, the Republicans were victorious. Mr. Cleveland had been re-nominated, but was defeated by the Hon. Benjamin Harrison. Mr. Roosevelt had cordially supported the Republican ticket, and his friends thought him highly fitted to be Assistant Secretary of State. In his interval of private life, Mr. Roosevelt had again traveled abroad; he was intelligently interested in foreign affairs, and he would have been a valuable man in the Secretary of State's office at a time when a number of foreign ques-

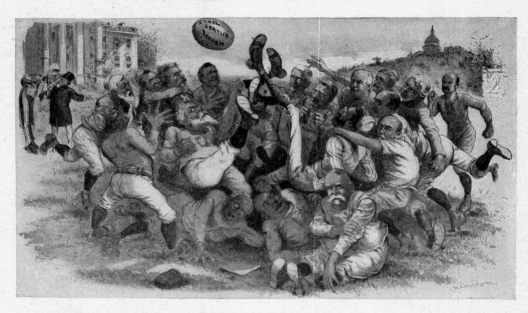

POLITICAL FOOTBALL

President Harrison: "What can *I* do when both parties insist on kicking?"

From *Judge*, 1889 (New York)

The Mob of Hungry Office-Seekers: "Harrison holds the fort."

Cleveland: "Aha! Now you know how it is yourself, Ben!"

From *Judge*, 1889 (New York)

STRAWS THAT BREAK THE CAMEL'S BACK

HARRISON: "I can make no progress with public business until I get rid of that load of straw."

From *Judge*, April 6, 1889

tions of some moment were pending. But Mr. Blaine, who had been an unsuccessful candidate for the nomination, was made Secretary of State, and he had not forgotten Roosevelt's attitude in the convention of 1884.

Mr. Harrison, therefore, found something else for the energetic young man from New York and Dakota. The new civil-service act was unpopular with the politicians of both parties. Yet every one realized that the spoils system had run its course, and that the great business of public administration had to be put upon some basis of merit, efficiency, and permanence. The enforcement of the act was not popular. No man of great political ambition, or high party standing, desired to be made a civil-service commissioner

From *Puck*. Copyright, 1889. By permission

DRAW YOUR OWN

(When Stanley carried the first steamboat up the Congo, the natives ran along the banks, yelling with rage,

CONCLUSIONS
and striving to check his progress by throwing stones and other missiles. Mr. Stanley got there, just the same.)

BOMBARDMENT OF THE WHITE HOUSE BY THE ARMY OF OFFICE SEEKERS
From *Judge*, April 8, 1893

Mr. Harrison, however, offered this seemingly thankless post of difficult service to Theodore Roosevelt, who promptly accepted it.

It should be remembered that from the time of James Buchanan to the time of Grover Cleveland, the Democrats had been out of office. Thus for the twenty-five years from 1861 to 1885 the Republicans had been filling the offices from top to bottom with their own men. The Democrats were hungry for their turn, and although President Cleveland was not in sympathy with the spoils system, he could not resist the pressure which put scores of thousands of Republican office-holders, great and small, into private life, in order to meet the clamoring of the Democrats for at least half of the salaried positions of the government. Furthermore, in the latter half of his term, Mr. Cleveland was a candidate for renomination; and he allowed himself to be guided by his political friends and supporters, and by the Democratic Na-

NO PLACE LIKE HOME—FOR OFFICE SEEKERS
From the *Wasp* (San Francisco), March 18, 1893

tional Committee, in much that had to do with appointments to office.

When, therefore, Mr. Harrison was elected in November, 1888, and entered upon his administration in March, 1889, it was natural enough that there should have been a furious onrush of Republican office-seekers. A large part of these were the indignant people who had been from time to time displaced during the brief four years of Democratic rule.

There were three Civil Service Commissioners, and Theodore Roosevelt was chairman of the board. The law did not prevent the dismissal of government employees, but it provided a system under which appointments were to be made upon merit, ascertained in chief part by examinations; and this system was under the control of the Civil Service Commissioners. The system was ridiculed and assailed. At each session of Congress there was a formidable attempt to starve out the system by refusing to appropriate the

UNCLE SAM'S DISMAL SWAMP
(It will have to be drained to get rid of the noxious miasmas that arise from it.)
From *Puck*, November 15, 1893

money necessary for the expenditures of the Civil Service Board.

Mr. Harrison was a good President, and instinctively in favor of a business-like public service; but he belonged to his own period and he was a candidate for a second term. The cabinet officers and the heads of bureaus, in large part, wanted to appoint their subordinates in their own way. They regarded the civil-service restrictions as irksome. Mr. Roosevelt at times stood practically alone, with the politicians and the more partisan newspapers against him. But public opinion would not permit the repeal of the civil-service law, and Roosevelt not only enforced it but secured its gradual extension, so that it applied to an ever-increasing number of public offices.

THEODORE ROOSEVELT AS HE LOOKED WHEN REAPPOINTED TO THE CIVIL SERVICE COMMISSION IN 1893

Mr. Cleveland and Mr. Harrison were again the opposing candidates in 1892, and the Democrats carried the day. Mr. Cleveland showed his appreciation of the chairman of the Civil Service Board by asking him to remain at his post, and Mr. Roosevelt consented. Again there was the pandemonium of office-seekers at Washington. The Democrats insisted that they were entitled to the spoils of their victory. Mr. Cleveland was in a position to stand more firmly than in his first term for the merit system, and he and Roosevelt found themselves working together for efficient and economical administration and against the evils of the spoils system,—just as they had been working together ten years before in the State of New York.

Mr. Roosevelt held this office for six continuous years, from 1889 to 1895. It was a period of patriotic service, with little promise of glory or reward. A man of different physical and nervous organization would have been worn out with the nagging and worry of a place that was involved in sharp, unceasing controversy. But the fights for the law, and against the politicians, did not worry Mr. Roosevelt in the least. He was able to keep it all within office hours, and it was a kind of work that gave him exceptional familiarity with every phase of the administrative system of the United States Government.

It gave him, also, a vast acquaintance with the personalities of Congress, and the active men in all branches of the government. Within a little more than six years it was his destiny to become President of the United States; and few experiences could have fitted him so well for the Presidency as the six years of firm, incessant battling at Washington for the systematizing of the government's work in all departments.

Copyright by G. G. Bain, N. Y.

Avery D. Andrews.   Mr. Parker.   Mr. Roosevelt.   Gen. Fred. D. Grant.

THE FOUR MEMBERS OF THE NEW YORK POLICE BOARD IN ROOSEVELT'S TIME (*See next chapter.*)

CHAPTER VI
Reforming New York's Police Work

THERE had been fruitless endeavors for many years, to elect a reform mayor and bring new methods and ideas into the municipal administration of New York City. Mr. Roosevelt had always believed, and said, that New York afforded a boundless field of usefulness for any man who chose to put his energies into its social or political service. At length, in the fall of 1894, all the anti-Tammany forces of the city had united upon a candidate and had elected as mayor Mr. William L. Strong, a merchant of public spirit and repute. Under the charter then existing, the principal function of the mayor was to select the heads of working departments.

The most difficult department on many accounts was that of the police. This department was charged with duties far more extensive than the control of some thousands of policemen in their work of maintaining law and order, and of aiding in the prevention and punishment of crime. The Police Department was charged with the enforcement of important laws of the State of New York that had to do with the manners and morals

PRESIDENT ROOSEVELT, OF THE NEW YORK POLICE COMMISSIONERS, LAYING DOWN THE LAW: "I would rather see this administration turned out because it enforced the laws than see it succeed by violating them."

From the *World* (New York)

AN AWFUL POSSIBILITY UNDER OUR BLUE LAWS AS ROOSEVELT ENFORCES THEM

From the *World* (New York)

FATHER KNICKERBOCKER: "Gracious! What next?"

From the *Herald* (New York)

COMMISSIONER ROOSEVELT AT HIS DESK
IN MULBERRY STREET (POLICE
HEADQUARTERS), NEW YORK

From a drawing made from life at the time for
the *Review of Reviews*

of the people. The Police Department,
further, had control over the tenement
house conditions, and at that time was
even more important than the Health
Department in its relations with the
sanitary and social welfare of the
people.

The charter called for a board of four
police commissioners, one of whom
should be the president of the board.
Mayor Strong asked Mr. Roosevelt to
return from Washington to become
chairman of the Board of Police Commissioners of his native city. To have
enforced the civil-service laws at
Washington was, in the estimation of
all politicians, to perform a work so
unpopular as to destroy a man's
chances of future preferment and

CIVILIZATION AND BARBARISM

" When we get in again we'll KEEP WIDE OPEN, and
SHUT UP THE CHURCHES—see ! "—From *Harper's Weekly.*

public honor. Now he was asked to take upon himself the work of Police Commissioner in New York City, with the intention of enforcing unpopular laws of the State, and of breaking up the blackmailing and grafting practices which had for so long a time prevailed in the Police Department—in partnership with the criminal elements on the one hand, and the mercenary politicians and large corporation interests on the other hand. To attack these evils was to attempt a task of Augean stable-cleaning that was more unwelcome and far more contentious and difficult than to be embroiled with the national politicians in attempts to enforce the civil-service law.

Mr. Roosevelt did not hesitate to accept this difficult office. The eyes of the country were upon him in his work, just as they had been when at Albany he was dealing with similar questions and problems. All the growing cities of America were wrestling with the difficulties of municipal reform. The police department in most cities seemed to be at the very

"THE LAW AND DUTY"—*Harper's Weekly*, July 17, 1895
(Roosevelt, as the Police Commissioner in New York, enforcing the Sunday closing law against strong opposition.)

center of civic misrule and corruption. Mr. Roosevelt's sympathies were with every policeman who tried to do his duty, and he recognized the fact that the corruption of the police force was due much more to the conditions outside than to those inside of the body of policemen. His discipline was severe, but he became popular with the rank and file of the city's uniformed guardians.

He had always been an optimist about our city populations. He explored the tenement houses, and in his brief two years as Police Commissioner he accomplished a great work in the destruction of unsanitary tenements and the improvement of housing conditions. He knew that most of the plain people were industrious and honest, and that the hordes of immigrants speaking many languages would rapidly become Americanized and make good citizens. He was striving in every way possible to improve their environment, in order that these people might contribute the more effectively toward the welfare and progress of the community.

A source of great evil and much blackmail had been the old laws of the State requiring the closing of business places, and particularly of licensed liquor saloons, on Sunday. The Sunday closing law was violated almost universally, but its existence gave opportunity for blackmail that at once corrupted the police force and intensified many other evils. Mr. Roosevelt took the ground that laws must be enforced or changed. He pressed his point so aggressively that Mayor Strong was alarmed and many good people opposed him. He worked under the further difficulty of a divided police board. But he made a great record that will live in the municipal life of New York.

His work, and that of Colonel Waring as Street Cleaning Commissioner, have resulted in a stupendous advancement in the comfort, health, and safety of the great population on Manhattan Island that lives more densely than any other city population in the world.

Fortunate progress in many directions has been made in the metropolis since Mayor Strong's administration. But in several of the departments,—notably those having to do with the daily life and comfort of the people,—the advance movement seems to have derived its great impulse from efforts made at that time with such ardor and intensity by department heads of whom Roosevelt and Waring were conspicuous types. All day at his desk Mr. Roosevelt was the decisive, untiring Commissioner of Police. It is the sort of office that no hesitant, indecisive man should ever try to fill. He was transferring good policemen to difficult precincts, disciplining bad ones, and sequestering indifferent ones to suburban beats. At night, Mr. Roosevelt was shaking up sleeping or loitering patrolmen; unexpectedly appearing in police stations; but more especially he was examining the conditions of the over-crowded tenement houses, in companionship with newspaper-men and reformers like Jacob A. Riis,—in consequence of which reforms of a sweeping nature have followed.

MR. ROOSEVELT'S IDEA OF HIS WORK AS A COMMISSIONER

| I know also the most incredible difficulties with which you have become surrounded. | We have greatly improved the standard of discipline. We have preserved complete order. | We have warred against crime and vice more effectively than ever before. | We have striven to make the police force the terror of the burglar. |

(Based on T. R.'s letter of resignation to Mayor Strong.)

From the *Herald* (New York)

CHAPTER VII

Preparing the Navy for War

MR. ROOSEVELT'S duties as Police Commissioner did not prevent his taking an active part in the Presidential campaign of 1896 between Mr. McKinley and Mr. Bryan. The great issue was that of the monetary standards, and Mr. Roosevelt opposed the Bryan doctrine of the free coinage of silver with an energy that came near leading him to a misunderstanding of the honest motives of many Western people whose virtues in a general way he understood so well. Though not a technical political economist, or an authority in matters of monetary science and finance, Mr. Roosevelt's clear and well-trained mind led him to the firm grasp of sound principles.

There was still work for him to do in the fight for municipal reform in New York; but the national conditions

Copyright by Clinedinst, Washington

MR. ROOSEVELT IN THE NAVY DEPARTMENT

A HARD RACE AGAINST TIME

From the *Herald* (New York)

drew him again to Washington. Even before Mr. Cleveland went out of office in March, 1897, there was a high and ever-rising tide of American public opinion that demanded our intervention in Cuba for the sake of ending an intolerable situation. Our commercial relations with Cuba were intimate and important. Spanish administration had been selfish, corrupt, and detrimental to Cuba's welfare.

From the time when most of Spanish America had established its independence early in the Nineteenth Century, Cuban revolutions had occurred one after another, only to be suppressed. But in 1895 a Cuban revolt occurred

MR. ROOSEVELT AS ASSISTANT SECRETARY OF THE NAVY

From the *World* (New York)

that was managed with skill and was prepared for a long struggle. With Cuba lying so near our coasts, and with a good many American adventurers helping the insurgents, while arms and ammunition were constantly smuggled into Cuba from this country as a base of supplies, the situation between our government and that of Spain had grown very critical, when Mr. McKinley was inaugurated in March, 1897.

The Hon. John D. Long, of Massachusetts, was made Secretary of the Navy, and Mr. Roosevelt, who had felt strongly the necessity of Spanish withdrawal from Cuba, and the importance of naval preparation on our part, was willing enough to take the post of assistant secretary. The New York political machine stood in the way at first, but Senator Platt's reluctant consent was given at length, and on April 6 Mr. Roosevelt was duly appointed Assistant Secretary of the Navy. It was understood that in that post he was to be the active executive officer of the department.

It must not be forgotten that our navy at that time was low in rank and that European naval authorities considered the Spanish navy stronger in ships, equipment and men than ours. There was real fear lest, if trouble came, Spain's European fleet might attack the Atlantic seaboard, while her Asiatic fleet, with headquarters at Manila, might occupy Honolulu as a re-coaling base and attack San Francisco.

MR. ROOSEVELT AS ASSISTANT SECRETARY OF THE NAVY
From the *World* (New York)

Mr. Roosevelt's early studies were of use to him in his new post. His preparation of the volume on our naval war of 1812 had led him into a broad reading of naval history. He had been recognized in Europe as a naval writer, and had been associated with Captain Mahan in certain contributions to a history of naval warfare. His remarkable energy had found precisely the work that was most congenial at the moment. He cultivated the society of the ablest naval officers in Washington, and found

AMERICA AND SPAIN PREPARING FOR A NAVAL WAR
From *El Ahuizote* (Mexico)

out what was most necessary to be done.   He had to fight against apathy and red-tape everywhere.

It has been characteristic of Mr. Roosevelt at all times that he has known whom to consult, and where and how to find out what things should be done.   And, having found out, he has had the force and energy to do those things without hesitation and with surprising promptness.

We have on record a little statement of his own which pictures the things he found to do while Assistant Secretary of the Navy:

"Commodore Dewey, Captain Evans, Captain Brownson, Captain Davis,—with these and the various other naval officers on duty at Washington, I used to hold long consultations, during which we went over and over not only every question of naval administration but specifically everything necessary to do in order to put the navy in trim to strike quick and hard if, as we believed to be the case, we went to war with Spain.   Sending an ample quantity of ammunition to the Asiatic squadron and providing it with coal; getting the battleships and the armored cruisers on the Atlantic into one squadron, both to train them in maneuvering together, and to have them ready to sail against either the Cuban or the Spanish coasts; gathering the torpedo boats into a flotilla for practice; securing ample target exercise, so conducted as to raise the standard of our marksmanship; gathering in the small ships from European and South American waters; settling on the number and kind of craft needed as auxiliary cruisers,—every one of these points was threshed over in conversations with officers who were present in Washington, or in correspondence with officers who, like Captain Mahan, were absent."

If, at the moment, in some of this work Mr. Roosevelt's energy was not appreciated by his superiors in the McKinley administration, or by older naval officers who had fallen into easy-going habits, it was approved by the country as a whole; and its wisdom was destined to be admitted by everybody before the mid-summer of 1898.   The late Senator Cushman K. Davis, who was at that time chairman of the Committee on Foreign Relations, declared that "If it had not been for Roosevelt, Dewey would not have been able to strike the blow that he dealt at Manila.   Roosevelt's sagacity, energy, and promptness saved us."

THE NAVY IS READY
From the *Criterion* (New York), May, 1898.

CHAPTER VIII

The Rough Rider of 1898

IN the opening sentences of his volume, "The Rough Riders," Mr. Roosevelt says that, while his party was still out of power, he had preached with all the fervor and zeal he possessed " our duty to intervene in Cuba and to take this opportunity of driving the Spaniard from the Western world." And he goes on as follows:

" Now that my party had come to power, I felt it incumbent on me, by word and deed, to do all I could to secure the carrying out of the policy in which I so heartily believed; and from the beginning I had determined that, if a war came, somehow or other, I was going to the front. Meanwhile, there was any amount of work at hand in getting ready the navy, and to this I devoted myself."

War was declared in April, 1898. The navy was as nearly ready as it could be made. Armies can be somehow improvised, but navies require planning in advance. When wars break out, naval direction must pass over practically to the strategists and to the high naval officers. Thus Mr. Roosevelt felt that his period of especial usefulness at the naval office would have an end.

The army of the United States consisted of scattered companies and fragments of regiments, located at posts and garrisons extending across a continent and comprising altogether only about 25,000 men. It is within bounds to say that for a great many years previous to the Spanish war, no officer had commanded,—even for the drills, maneuvers and marching of peaceful days,—as many United States troops as would be comprised in three full regiments. The Spaniards in their struggle against the Cuban insurrection had massed in that island about 100,000 troops, transported from Spain. It was evident that

THE ROUGH RIDERS BRINGING THEIR DYNAMITE GUN INTO ACTION

THE ROUGH RIDERS ON A PRACTICE CHARGE

we should have to do something more than gather together the scattered fragments of our regular army. It was necessary to issue a call for volunteer troops, and this President McKinley did very promptly.

At first, Mr. Roosevelt thought of going to the front as a member of the staff of one of the generals; but some obstacle intervened, and when it was proposed to form a volunteer cavalry regiment or two from the cowboys and horsemen of the Western plains, Mr. Roosevelt had an opportunity to form such an organization and to become its colonel. He had, however, been much in company with an army surgeon, Dr. Leonard Wood, then residing in Washington, and he and Dr. Wood had found themselves in entire harmony regarding the Cuban question and the military situation. Dr. Wood had served in campaigns against the Apache Indians, where he had won credit and honor. It was arranged that Dr. Wood should be colonel and Mr. Roosevelt lieutenant-colonel of the First United States Volunteer Cavalry. Dr. Wood was slated for early promotion to a brigadier-generalship, and the regiment from the beginning was known as " Colonel Roosevelt's Rough Riders."

It was a very picturesque organization, and remarkable in the individual efficiency of its members. It was made up of cowboys from Montana to New Mexico and Arizona, Texas rangers, young Southern horsemen and young college men of the East who were accustomed to riding and shooting and fond of adventure. The regiment arrived in Cuba in time to participate in the brief but very real campaign near Sanitago, and Mr. Roosevelt

COL. THEODORE ROOSEVELT, OF THE ROUGH RIDERS

acquitted himself in a soldierly way that was quite in keeping with qualities that had been developed by the accumulated experiences of his life. In his earlier New York experience he had been a member of a militia company, and he had been accustomed to horses and firearms from school boy days.

The expansion of the army was sudden, and we were quite unprepared at Washing-

ROUGH RIDERS OF THE FALL OF 1898
From *Judge* (New York)

ton to manage it well on the business side. Many volunteers died in unsanitary camps who had no chance to go near the seat of war. Commissary supplies were mismanaged, our soldiers in Cuba were badly fed and supplied, and we were obliged to face serious scandals. Mr. Roosevelt's experience in Cuba gave him intimate knowledge of these conditions, and his protests helped to bring about some drastic reforms.

Soon after the war was over Mr. Elihu Root became Secretary of War, and there followed a thoroughgoing reform in army administration. Meanwhile it was a remarkable coincidence that a man who was destined so soon to become President of the United States, and therefore commander-in-chief of the army and navy, should have served at a critical time in the Navy Department and should have taken part conspicuously as a soldier at the front in the work of the army. The story of the Rough

THE ROUGH RIDERS
They are rough on the Spaniards, whether they ride or walk.

Riders is a fascinating book, and Roosevelt's name, more than that of any other participant, will remain associated with the war for the liberation of Cuba.

"WE HAVE DISCOVERED IN MR. ROOSEVELT THE MISSING LINK"
(Acceptable to Platt and the machine on one hand and to Choate, Low, and the reform wing on the other.)
From the *World* (New York)

CHAPTER IX

As Candidate for Governor

IT was in the month of August, 1898, that the troops came back from Cuba in bad condition from improper food and supplies, and were encamped for restoration in the bracing air of Montauk Point at the eastern end of Long Island. There the Rough Riders remained until they were mustered out and disbanded on September 15.

The people of New York were about to enter upon a gubernatorial campaign. The Republicans were charged with having made dishonest use of money appropriated for the enlargement of the State canals. The so-called "Raines Law" had provided for turning the saloons of

INFORMATION FOR THE COLONEL
BOSS PLATT TO COL. ROOSEVELT: "It's a cinch, Teddy."
From the *Herald* (New York)

43

PLATT AS CYRANO DE BERGERAC
From the *World* (New York)

ROOSEVELT'S CONDITION—AN UNCONDITIONAL
BY THE REPUBLICAN MACHINE
From *Puck*.   Copyright 1898.   By permission.

New York into sham hotels to evade the Sunday closing law, and great abuse and scandal had resulted. There was just criti-cism of the management of the State insur-ance department, as well as that of public works. Mr. Platt was at the height of his sway as Republican boss, and his followers had in so far abused their privileges of office

EDITING THE COLONEL
(No. 49 Broadway was Mr. Platt's business address, from
which he was supposed to direct the campaign.)
From the *World* (New York)

SIGNOR TEDDI'S DARING ATTEMPT
(This double load can't be carried to Albany.)
From the *Journal* (New York)

"BEWARE OF THE GREEK BEARING GIFTS"
(Boss Platt as leading the Trojan horse.)
From the *World* (New York)

could not forget the political crisis of 1884, and he was reluctant to take any position that could put him outside the ranks of the Republican party. He agreed under certain circumstances to accept an independent nomination, but he proposed not to be a candidate until after he had had a fair chance to see what his own party was going to do. Mr. Platt and his chief lieutenants were thoroughly opposed to Roosevelt, but they were facing certain defeat if they put any man known to be identified with themselves at the head of the ticket. The alternative was bitter for them, but they accepted Roosevelt.

He ran as a straight Re-

and power that they were facing an almost inevitable defeat at the polls.

It looked like an opportunity for the Democratic machine; and the Independents, together with many Republicans and Democrats of high personal standing, were thinking it necessary to nominate a third candidate against the machine tickets of the two parties. Mr. Roosevelt had every qualification by his previous experiences to lead such a movement; besides which his fresh popularity as colonel of the Rough Riders, and the hero of San Juan, was sure to add to his strength as a vote getter.

Colonel Roosevelt, however,

"NO TIME FOR SLUMBER"
(The Colonel arouses his apathetic party.)
From the *Herald* (New York)

THE ROUGH RIDER'S LATEST CHARGE
From the *World* (New York)

HYPNOTIZED BY PLATT AS SVENGALI
" He wept with delight when Platt gave him a smile,
And trembled with fear at his frown."
From the *Journal* (New York)

BAGGED HIS GAME
From the *Tribune* (Minneapolis)

publican and gave his cordial support to the
other names on the Republican ticket. The
cartoonists were much concerned through
the campaign with his relations to Senator
Platt as the acknowledged leader of the
party in the State. Mr. Roosevelt's own
point of view was clear on all such points.
He would accept no man's dictation in anything that concerned his freedom of opinion
or utterance, or his responsible actions as
governor in case of his election. But in all
things where custom and propriety allowed
him to act as a member of his party he was
prepared to consult cordially and fully with
those who were the official heads and leaders of the party organization. He was willing to listen to suggestions from such leaders as to appointments to office, but would
appoint no man to any position unless he
was convinced of the man's honesty and
faithfulness, and of his entire fitness to perform the duties of the place in question.

In his campaign Mr. Roosevelt was entirely frank as respects administrative scandals. He promised to unearth the canal
frauds if any were to be found, and to deal

THE CHAMPION ROUGH RIDER OF THE WORLD.

From the *Evening Post* (Denver)

as unsparingly with wrong-doers of the Republican party as if they were members of the opposing organization. Up to this time he had not had much experience as a public speaker, and the leaders were strongly opposed to his taking the stump in his own behalf. But the campaign began apathetically, and Mr. Roosevelt, with his unfailing instinct for the dramatic, took a few of his cowboys with him, allowed them to tell the public what they thought of their Colonel, and the Rough Riders drew the crowds, to whom the Colonel appealed with his direct promises to introduce reform wherever needed. He was elected by a plurality of about 17,000 in a year when a less striking candidate must have been defeated by a large Democratic plurality.

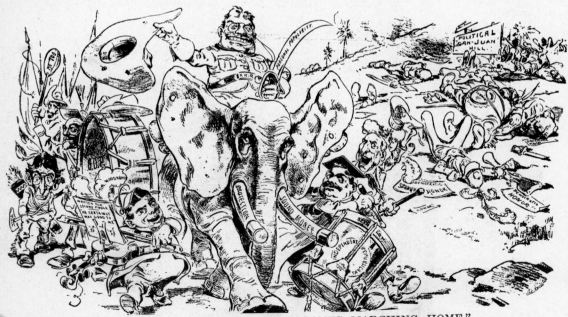

"AND TEDDY (ROOSEVELT) COMES MARCHING HOME"

From *Judge* (New York)

CHAPTER X
In the Gubernatorial Chair

HON. THEODORE ROOSEVELT
(As Governor of New York)

MR. ROOSEVELT began his term as governor with a message to the legislature that was ringing and statesmanlike. The people had elected a Republican governor charged with the duty of reforming conditions that the Republicans themselves had brought about. Governor Roosevelt appointed Democratic lawyers, together with engineering and financial experts, to examine into the expenditures of the canal millions. The Department of Public Works was reorganized on a practical business basis with proper men in charge.

In the other departments of the State government, the process of shifting things from a political to a business basis was quietly but firmly carried out. Great improvements were made in managing charitable and penal institutions. The insurance department and the bank department, under control of the governor of New York, have to supervise the insurance companies, and the banks and trust companies, that are the most essential and important of any in the nation. The work of these departments was reorganized by Governor Roosevelt, though the task cost him a stubborn fight.

A board of revision was appointed to give New York an improved charter in view of

"JUST WATCH ME, TEDDY!"
(Mr. Platt essaying to subdue the legislative bronco.)
From the *World* (New York)

PLATT'S POLITICAL CEMETERY
From the *World* (New York)

GOVERNOR ROOSEVELT'S RINGING MESSAGE TO THE LEGISLATURE
(At the beginning of his term as Governor of New York.)
From the *World* (New York)

the recent consolidation of New York and Brooklyn. The educational work of the State was improved, and in many ways the social welfare of the people of the Empire State was advanced under Mr. Roosevelt's administration.

The subject that proved in the end to have been the most influential in its bearing upon Mr. Roosevelt's future career was that of State taxation. During his early months as governor, a State senator, the Hon. John Ford, introduced a bill designed to secure for the State a proper revenue from public-service corporations, such as street railway companies and gas and electric lighting companies, which were in the enjoyment of unlimited and perpetual franchises. The

ROOSEVELT: "Hands off, Tommy! I'll do the driving!"
(Roosevelt decides at the very start to be an un unbossed Governor, though accused of obeying Platt.)
From the *Herald* (New York)

GOVERNOR ROOSEVELT SHEARING THE PUBLIC FRANCHISES SHEEP WITH THE FRANCHISE TAX SHEARS, TO THE DISMAY OF MR. PLATT

The three cartoons on this page are from the *World* (New York)

THE BOSS'S ANXIETY

Mr. Platt to Governor Roosevelt: "You wouldn't rob the Old Man, would you?"

(Mr. Platt sees the possibility of campaign contributions from the corporations being diverted from the party by the proposed franchise tax.)

A CRITICAL MOMENT FOR BOTH

(Mr. Platt trying to lead the broncho, Governor Roosevelt, into the corporation paddock, during the extra session of the Legislature called to deal with the matter of a franchise tax.)

"NO CHOICE BETWEEN ROTTEN APPLES"

(The apples stand for the Franchise tax; one is
labeled "Roosevelt plan," the other "Ford plan"—
both equally distasteful to Mr. Platt, the marketman.)
From the *World* (New York)

PLATT'S TUMULTUOUS TIMES WITH TEDDY

PLATT, THE "EASY BOSS'S," LATEST UTTERANCE:
"Peace is beautiful, but visionary. It is not for this
age."
From the *World* (New York)

street railway lines, particularly those of New York City, had been formed into a vast monopoly, capitalized at hundreds of millions of dollars by the issuing of inflated securities.

Most of the issues of stocks and bonds were based upon the commercial value of these
franchises, rather than upon tangible property. Senator Ford held that such franchises
ought to be assessed at their market value, just as real estate is assessed for purposes of
taxation.

Public opinion and the best newspapers supported him, and Governor Roosevelt

RECEIVING A LESSON IN HARMONY

(Mr. Platt, who had some talent for harmony, both
musical and political, is here shown as giving Roosevelt a lesson.)
From the *Herald* (New York)

IN AMBUSH FOR THE ROUGH RIDER

(Croker with a club labeled "To hell with reform," and Platt with one labeled "The public be
damned.")
From the *World* (New York)

TEDDY TO THE RESCUE OF REPUBLICANISM

(The importance to the Republican party of the Ohio campaign of 1899, for its bearing on the nomination of President McKinley for a second term, caused the party managers to draft a large number of distinguished office-holders, including Governor Roosevelt, of New York, for speeches in that State.)

From the *Verdict* (New York), October 30, 1899

THE CANAL STEAL PUZZLE

Will Governor Roosevelt interpose between fraud and justice (in the matter of the expenditure of the Barge Canal appropriation)?

From the *Verdict* (New York), January 2, 1899

ROOSEVELT'S IDEA OF REORGANIZATION

(Governor Roosevelt dealing with the question of the reorganization of the Police Department of New York City.)

From the *Verdict* (New York), March 13, 1899

EXCELSIOR TEDDY

"Try not the Pass, the Old Man said."

(Mr. Roosevelt desired a second term as Governor. The nomination "Pass," however, was guarded by his political enemies—hence Mr. Platt's warning.)

From the *Verdict* (New York)

THE STATE SENATE HAS TURNED TURTLE, SWAMPING THE TUG REFORM

From the *Herald* (New York)

"LOOK OUT FOR THE COP!"
(Tammany Hall trying to rush a rapid transit plan through "Legislature Avenue." Roosevelt, as the cop, ready to smite it when it comes up for his approval at Governor Street.)

From the *World* (New York)

gave Senator Ford the backing of his support in so far as the principles involved in the Ford bill were concerned. Senator Platt's Republican machine and Mr. Croker's Tammany machine were alike opposed to the Ford scheme of taxing corporation franchises. Both political organizations derived a great part of their pecuniary support from the contributions they were accustomed to exact from the very set of corporations which it was proposed to tax under the Ford scheme.

Mr. Roosevelt was urged in high and influential quarters not to support any form of franchise tax. But he stood by the plan, called an extra session of the legislature, and with the masses of the people behind him, put the bill through the Senate and Assembly, gave it his signature, and made it a law. This action was typical of his brilliant administration as governor.

When the legislature assembly in January, 1900, Governor Roosevelt presented to it an annual message of great scope and statesmanlike ability, in which he discussed the problem of commercial monopolies and so-called trusts, and dealt broadly with the policies in which it seemed to him the State of New York should point the way for other commonwealths. He was looking forward to renomination as governor in the autumn of that year, in order that in a second term of two years he might complete the program he had laid out for himself as chief of the government of the State of New York.

He breaketh loose from college

He turneth up his toes in the race for Mayor

He cow-puncheth

He worketh the Civil Service racket

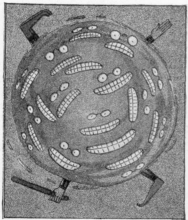

He maketh the Police Board like unto a dentist's shop

He becometh part of the whole thing in the Navy Department

He leadeth Rough Riders who never rode

He announceth independence of Platt

He giveth the jay information about the canal steal

He worketh the tread-mill for T. Platt

THE CAREER OF TEDDY.—From the *Verdict* (New York), November 6, 1899

CHAPTER XI

Named for the Vice-Presidency

FOR American politicians, the issues of a Presidential year overshadow all other affairs of a public nature. The year 1900 was one of much political excitement. We had acquired the Philippines as one result of the war with Spain. Mr. Bryan and the Democrats were attacking the McKinley administration on the new issue of imperialism. Many people besides the Democrats were criticising the administration because of Secretary Alger's unpopular management of the War Department. Governor Roosevelt was stoutly defending the expansion policy, and our acquisitions in the Atlantic and Pacific, but he was well known to be critical of the War Department. The State Department had blundered frightfully with the original Hay-Pauncefote Treaty, and Roosevelt had openly denounced it and helped to prevent its ratification.

The administration in turn was not devotedly attached to Governor Roosevelt, and Secretary Alger had failed to show appreciation of the war record of the gallant colonel

A PAGE FROM ROOSEVELT'S "CROMWELL"

(Governor Roosevelt's hardest personal fight had to do with the removal of Louis F. Payn, a well-known politician, as State Superintendent of Insurance.)

EXECUTIONER PLATT (to Teddy the Leveler): "I pray thee, remember 1904. Thine intended victim [Payn] is somewhat of a leveler himself."

From the *Verdict* (New York)

THE TWO TEDDY ROOSEVELTS

HE WASN'T AFRAID { To be independent of Platt, To punish canal thieves, To refuse the Vice-Presidency;

BUT { He hasn't been independent of Platt, He let the thieves get away, And he's breaking his neck for the Vice-Presidency;

BECAUSE HE'S AFRAID OF PLATT

From the *Verdict* (New York)

"HERE, HERE, WHAT'S THIS?"

(Mr. Platt conferring with Roosevelt about the Presidential nomination for 1900. President McKinley, himself a candidate for renomination, appears as an interested listener.)

From the *World* (New York)

of the Rough Riders. It was supposed that the Secretary was endeavoring to keep Mr. Roosevelt's name off the list of those to whom Congress was voting medals of honor.

No President ever approaches the time of his renomination without discovering that there are numerous people who would prefer to try a new candidate. Many critics of the administration were proposing to deprive McKinley of a second term, and to nominate Roosevelt at Philadelphia in 1900. The more practical party managers, however, saw that the logic of the situation called for a second McKinley term.

The friends and admirers of Mr. Roosevelt were planning to elect him in the fall of

TROUBLE WITH THE PHILIPPINE BRONCHO

UNCLE SAM: "Say, Mr. McKinley, why don't you get a professional like Roosevelt to ride that broncho?"—From the *Herald* (New York)

"THE LIGHT AND SHADOW OF 1900"

(Roosevelt is represented as the rising sun of 1900, while Alger and the army scandals throw a shadow over President McKinley.)

From the *Herald* (New York)

SECRETARY ALGER: "You're one of the round-robins; you don't get a medal."

(Colonel Roosevelt with other officers in Cuba had sent a "round-robin" letter to the War Department protesting against bad commissary supplies and retention of sick in service, and this had been regarded as a breach of military discipline.)—From the *Herald* (New York)

THE VICE-PRESIDENCY

ROOSEVELT: "What! Me? Never! I'll be the whole show or nothin'!"

From the *Herald* (New York)

THE ROUGH RIDER'S EYES ON THE WHITE HOUSE

From the *Herald* (New York)

IS HE SETTING THE SWITCH FOR THE ROOSEVELT FLYER?

From the *Tribune* (New York)

1900 to a second term as governor, and to bring him forward as their Presidential candidate in 1904. Mr. Roosevelt's enemies, however, had a different program. The Vice-Presidency had always been regarded as a somewhat empty honor and as a place for disposing of men who were not wanted in active politics. The corporations that had opposed the franchise tax, and that were very close to the Republican boss, Senator Platt, were determined to have some other man for governor. Roosevelt was too strong to be defeated in a direct fight. The only plan they could devise was to have him run for Vice-President on the ticket with Mr. McKinley.

"NAY, NAY!"

From the *World* (New York)

THE MAN ON HORSEBACK

From the *World* (New York)

"Yes, Willie, here is a nice little boy Nursie and I have found to play with you. Treat him kindly, as he is very timid and retiring."

"What ails you, Willie?"
"Look at that campaign banner that Teddy has painted!"

"Goodness me, Willie, what ails you this time?"
"We're playing Republican Campaign Trip, and Teddy's making all the speeches from the rear platform, and he says I'm merely a brakeman."

"Yes, Willie, Nursie has to suppress Teddy when his rich uncle is visiting us. He says too many foolish things."

(These clever cartoons by Mr. Frederick B. Opper appeared in a series entitled "Willie and His Papa, and the Rest of the Family," published in the New York *Evening Journal* during the years 1900 and 1901. "Willie" referred to President McKinley, "Papa" was the Trusts, "Nursie" represented Mr. Hanna, while the active little figure in the Rough Rider costume stood, of course, for the irrepressible "Teddy." Other prominent personalities, comprising the "Rest of the Family," were occasionally introduced by Mr. Opper into the drawings of the series.)

COMPARISONS ARE ODIOUS
(Why Hanna does not want Teddy riding behind Mc-Kinley in 1900.)

From the *Verdict* (New York), January 1, 1900

CUTTING OUT THE YEARLING
TEDDY: "I must get my own brand on this calf before he gets into the Trust Herd."

(Referring to Mr. Roosevelt's aspirations for the Presidential nomination of 1904.)

From the *Verdict* (New York), May 7, 1900

TEDDY BESIEGED
With a liberal supply of gubernatorial mule meat, he may be able to hold out till 1904.

(Governor Roosevelt, being pressed by Platt and Quay to accept the Vice-Presidential nomination of 1900, in order to eliminate him from active politics.)

From the *Verdict* (New York), May 14, 1900

THE TAIL OF THE PRESIDENTIAL KITE
(The "Rough Rider" tail to the McKinley kite of 1900.)

From the *Verdict* (New York), July 9, 1900

GOVERNOR ROOSEVELT IN THE CONVENTION

(Senator Depew is on the extreme left, and the other three standing figures are Governor Roosevelt, Dr. Leslie D. Ward, and Hon. B. B. Odell, Jr. Senator Platt's face is partly shown in the lower right-hand corner. The illustration is from one of the remarkable convention photographs taken by the New York *Tribune*, by whose courtesy we use it.)

As early as February, Governor Roosevelt had issued a frank statement saying that under no circumstances would he accept a nomination to the Vice-Presidency, and declaring his desire to serve the people of New York in a second term as governor. He went to the Philadelphia convention as chairman of the delegates from New York. The street railroad magnates had arranged, through Senator Quay, to have Pennsylvania lead in the movement to make Roosevelt the Vice-Presidential candidate. Mr. McKinley and his manager, Senator Hanna, had other plans, but there was an insistent demand for Roosevelt from the Western States where Bryan was very strong. Many of these Western delegates asserted openly that they were prepared to abandon McKinley and make Roosevelt the head of the ticket. The pressure became irresistible and Mr. Roosevelt finally abandoned his preference.

Messrs. Platt, Quay, and the corporations had undoubtedly started the movement. They would not have prevailed, however, but for the genuine Roosevelt sentiment in the West. Roosevelt accepted the nomination for the Vice-Presidency not at the hands of his enemies, but at the hands of his friends. He felt that he was giving up his best chance for usefulness, as well as his probable future preferment. But it seemed to be his duty, and it was always Mr. Roosevelt's way to try to face the immediate emergency in honorable fashion and let the future take care of itself.

ROOSEVELT CANNOT GET AWAY FROM THIS STAMPEDE, LED BY PENNSYLVANIA
From the *Inquirer* (Philadelphia)

At almost every stage in his career he had illustrated the principle that the best way to save one's life is to seem to lose it at the call of duty. The New York political machine chuckled and sneered, and the enemies that Roosevelt had made through his honest and vigorous administration as governor thought that Samson was shorn of his locks. If Mr. Roosevelt's friends were a little disheartened, the governor himself was cheerful and buoyant. He had done his best, he was still young, and very much interested in the passing show, and he had never allowed himself to be the victim of ambition.

ROUNDED UP
(Expressing the belief that the bosses had captured Roosevelt)
From the *Journal* (New York)

CHAPTER XII

His First National Stumping Tour

SENATOR MARK HANNA, of Ohio, who was President McKinley's close friend and political manager, was at this time chairman of the National Republican Committee. Mr. Bryan, (who had also volunteered in the Spanish war, and had been made a colonel of volunteers, though he had not reached the front) was again the Democratic nominee for the Presidency. He was the most skilful and assiduous campaign speaker in the country. His chances for election were not regarded as by any means hopeless.

THE TAIL NOW THREATENS TO WAGGLE THE DOG
From the *Times-Democrat* (New Orleans)

MARCUS AURELIUS (HANNA) TO THEODORIUS: "That general [Apathy] must be ousted, or we'll fall without the breastworks."

From the *Times* (Minneapolis)

STANDING BY THE PRESIDENT
From the *World* (New York)

Many of the best minds of the country, Republicans as well as Democrats, were profoundly opposed to the policy of acquiring the Philippines, with its attendant reorganization of the army and navy on a permanent scale of great costliness, and its inevitable sequel of new and untried adventures as a world power. Some one had to defend these policies on the stump, in a telling way, on behalf of the Republican ticket. Mr. Roosevelt, by common consent and demand, was the man to speak for his party.

He had, while serving his first year as governor, made a notable address before the Hamilton Club at Chicago,—not a stump harangue, but a carefully written oration,—in championship of the doctrine that the United States had grown into a maturity of influence and power which required the assumption of a full share of responsibility for the affairs of the world at large. In his earlier years, Mr. Roosevelt, as we have said, had not been an accomplished public speaker. He had been forcible and direct as a debater in the New York legislature, but he was not an orator, and had none of those easy gifts and tricks of speech so common among American politicians and so highly developed by the professional platform orators of Mr. Bryan's type.

BRANDED, BUT NOT BROKEN
From *Puck*. Copyright, 1900. By permission

THE WILD EASTERN TERROR IN THE MILD WEST
From the *Chronicle* (Chicago)

APPROACHING NEBRASKA
BRYAN: "That looks like a bad storm coming."
From the *Journal* (Minneapolis)

THE UNMUZZLED TEDDY RUNS AMUCK!

(Referring to some utterances of Governor Roosevelt in the Presidential campaign of 1900.)

From the *Verdict* (New York), August 6, 1900

THE "ROUGH" IDEA IN POLITICS

TEDDY: "Ah! just what was needed to carry out the effect."

(Mr. Roosevelt's speech at Cripple Creek was interrupted by a mob that threw missiles of all sorts)

From the *Evening News* (Detroit)

THE POLITICAL LOCHINVAR'S SUCCESSFUL
RIDE.

From the *Journal* (Minneapolis)

Mr. Roosevelt had improved, however, in this regard, not so much through practice or through taking thought as to his platform manner or diction, as through the maturing of his convictions and knowledge and the corresponding increase in the value and range of the things he had to say. It is usually the case that the man who is on the one hand a student and on the other hand a man of action, will succeed well enough in public debate or on the stump when real occasions present themselves.

Thus Governor Roosevelt in his capacity as "running mate" with President McKinley made a great speaking campaign throughout the United States in the summer and autumn of 1900. He was aided by his splendid physical vitality; and his speaking grew more effective day after day. He was never lacking in that mysterious attribute of magnetic per-

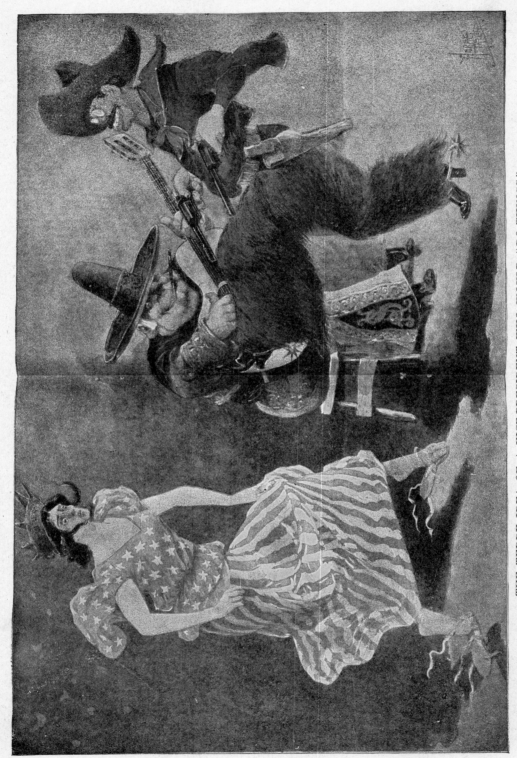

THE TEDDY IDEA OF A VICE-PRESIDENT WHO WOULD "DO THINGS"

(A pictorial reflection of a notion that prevailed quite generally to the effect that Colonel Roosevelt,—in case of his election to the Vice-Presidency,—would enliven that proverbially sedate and obscure office with his characteristic strenuousness.)

From the *Verdict* (New York), October 29, 1900

THE PROGRESS OF THE CAMPAIGN—ROOSEVELT
STUMPING IN THE WEST
From the *Times* (Washington)

MARK (HANNA) LEADING TEDDY
From the *News* (Chicago)

sonality that brings audiences together, and keeps them attentive to the speaker's words.

And his honesty and sincerity, together with the strength of his convictions, were bound to impress his audiences. There are some men who can never carry with them a campaign audience, because of their own lack of party spirit and because certain quali- ties of mind compel them to see both sides at once, so that they cannot lose the impartial and judicial spirit of history. They are hampered by philosophic doubts. Mr. Roosevelt, though a profound historical student, was even more the born fighter and the man of action.

His mind was always decisive. The issue before him took on ethical aspects, and he saw his own side clearly right and the other side essentially wrong.

To the group of anti-imperialists, Mr. Roosevelt's doctrines were abhorrent. Their timid, narrow, negative point of view was equally abhorrent to his bold and positive mind.

Mr. Roosevelt made a tour in that campaign of 22,000 miles, made five or six hun- dred speeches of considerable length, was the notable figure of the season,—as he had been of the Philadelphia convention,—directly addressed from 3,000,000 to 4,000,000 peo- ple, and in the course of four months had placed himself in the rank of the half-dozen most effective platform and campaign speakers in the entire political history of the country.

THE M'KINLEY   THE DEWEY   THE ROOSEVELT   THE BRYAN

LEADING FALL STYLES OF HEAD-WEAR FOR THE YEAR 1900.—From the *Eagle* (Brooklyn, N. Y.)

CHAPTER XIII

A Half-Year as Vice-President

AFTER the election early in November, Mr. Roosevelt had still to serve nearly two months as governor at Albany. He had then an interval of two months in which to prepare for changing his residence to Washington and assuming the dignities of the Vice-Presidency after the 4th of March. He quietly resumed his literary work (he had already written in 1898 his famous book, "The Rough Riders," and in 1899, while governor, had written a characteristic life of "Oliver Cromwell"), spent a much-needed winter vacation hunting the cougar, or mountain lion, in the Rocky Mountains, with pen as well as with gun, and reconciled himself to the prospects of four years of

OUR VICE-PRESIDENT-ELECT
From the *Times* (Washington)

THE ELECTION OF McKINLEY AND ROOSEVELT
G. O. P.: "Four—four—four years more."
From the *World* (New York)

PRESIDING OVER THE SENATE
From the *Post* (Washington)

WILLIE (McKINLEY) AND HIS PAPA (THE TRUSTS)

THE TRUSTS: "No, Teddy, you haven't got a living show for that piece of pie (the Presidential nomination of 1904); nursie (Hanna) has her eye on it."

From the Journal (New York)

SURE THING

"EASY BOSS" PLATT: "New York will furnish the next President."

ROOSEVELT
REED } —"I wonder if he means me!"
ODELL
ROOT

From the Journal (Minneapolis)

RUSHING THE BABY SHOW

UNCLE SAM: "You're altogether too early, ladies; the show doesn't open for a good while yet."

From the Journal (New York)

self-repressed, observant, and studious life in the functionless office of Vice-President.

The Senate was convened for a brief session in March to confirm the President's appointments. And thus Mr. Roosevelt had his opportunity to sit as its presiding officer for a few days. The regular session was not to begin until the first week in December, and it so happened that this brief experience in March completed his service as presiding officer of the Senate.

Already the politicians were looking forward to the year 1904. They

" Why, Willie, you seem angry. What is irritating you? "
" Teddy is getting up a ' Hall of Fame,' and I ain't in it."

" Crying again, Willie? What is it now? "
" Teddy isn't satisfied with riding his horse; he wants to ride the elephant, too."

" Well, well, Willie; what is it this time? "
" We're playing Republican minstrels, and Teddy wants to be the two end men and the middleman, too."

" What's the row here, Willie? "
" Teddy is going out to Meeker, Colorado, next week to shoot mountain lions, and he's practicing a little beforehand."

(Another group of cartoons taken from Mr. Opper's series of " Willie and His Papa." These also appeared in the *Evening Journal*, of New York, after the election of the McKinley-Roosevelt ticket in the fall of 1900, and during Mr. Roosevelt's brief period of service as Vice-President.)

supposed that Mr. Odell, or possibly ex-Speaker Reed (who had retired from Congress and had come to New York to practice law), might secure the support of the New York delegation and carry off the Presidential honors. Mr. Roosevelt, however, with no machine behind him, had won hosts of ardent friends throughout the country in typical groups, like the Hamilton Club, of Chicago, and other Western organizations. Many of those who had professed to be his close political friends in fair weather, had sought other political society. Among the time-serving politicians, Roosevelt's stock had declined to a low figure. Few men are so little able to discern the real signs of the times in American politics as the machine leaders. They know the rules of the game as they play it themselves, but the larger forces of public opinion are quantities that they can never estimate.

At the very time in July and August, 1901, when they were most certain that Mr. Roosevelt had been excluded from influence and power in the politics of his own State, and sidetracked from a career that would have led to the Presidency or to the Senate, the Roosevelt movement was, in fact, taking on strength and form throughout the whole country. Hosts of influential men were joining in it, though mainly without the cognizance of the old-fashioned professional politicians.

The men of the earlier political type could not understand that a new era had dawned

THE FOURTH OF MARCH, 1901

(A photograph taken on the day when Theodore Roosevelt was sworn in as Vice-President of the United States.)

in American affairs. With the rising men of a new generation, Roosevelt was stronger than any one else. These men had made it plain to Mr. Roosevelt that they were determined to control the national convention in his interest in 1904; and while he was taking no active steps himself, he could not refuse to listen and to observe.

Meanwhile Mr. Roosevelt was determined to be ready for whatever might happen. He resumed the reading of law that had been interrupted by his election to the legislature exactly twenty years before. His repute was such that he could not have failed at the end of four years in the Vice-Presidency to form connections that would enable him to earn an easy competence at the bar.

He laid out projects, moreover, for literary work; and proposed to use his sojourn in Washington and his seat in the presiding chair of the Senate to add every day to his already extraordinary knowledge of the men and the subjects about which a President ought to be well informed.

For a good while previous to the convention of 1900, the Vice-Presidency had as a rule been regarded with disfavor by men of ambition, and had usually been conferred upon men either of advanced years or comparative obscurity. Roosevelt's fame and position were already national, he had youth in his favor, and he could afford to take his chances in a great country where opportunities, whether in public or in private life, seemed well-nigh boundless.

REINCARNATION

(President Roosevelt making the statement: "It shall be my aim to continue absolutely unbroken the policy of President McKinley.")—From *Judge*.

CHAPTER XIV

Assuming the Presidency

IN September, 1901, Mr. Roosevelt was spending a few days in the wilderness of the Adirondacks. President McKinley had gone to Buffalo, New York, to visit the Pan-American Exposition and make an address. It was on September 6 that the country and the world were shocked by the news of the shooting of Mr. McKinley at the hands of an anarchist. Mr. Roosevelt was found and hurried to Buffalo, where the cabinet was gathered, awaiting the inevitable end.

Mr. McKinley died on the 14th, and Mr. Roosevelt at once took the oath of office at Buffalo. In Mr. McKinley's first term, Mr. Hobart, of New Jersey, had been Vice-President, and it had been Mr. McKinley's method to treat Mr. Hobart as a close personal and official adviser, rather than to hold him aloof. If Mr. Hobart had lived, he would have been renominated in 1900, and

HIS DECLARATION OF INDEPENDENCE

(Apropos of President Roosevelt's policy with regard to appointments to office.)

From *Puck*. Copyright, 1901. By permission

PUNCH, OR THE LONDON CHARIVARI.—September 25, 1901.

"THE ROUGH RIDER."

WITH MR. PUNCH'S BEST WISHES TO PRESIDENT ROOSEVELT.

VACCINATING THE TRUSTS

Give the doctor time; his patient has a lot of arms that need attention.

From the *Journal* (Minneapolis)

A GLIMPSE INTO THE FUTURE.—FAST AND TIGHT

(President Roosevelt endeavoring to regulate the trusts by proper Government control.)

From the *Pioneer Press* (St. Paul)

Mr. Roosevelt's career, however distinguished, must have been different in its external facts. When Mr. Roosevelt was selected at Philadelphia, Mr. McKinley promptly assured him that if the ticket should be elected, he would expect to treat Mr. Roose-

THE TARIFF-REVISION HORSE AND THE CONGRESSIONAL RIDER

PRESIDENT ROOSEVELT: "I could ride that critter, but I haven't any intention of trying it."

From the *Tribune* (Minneapolis)

THE ROUGH RIDER TO THE RESCUE

(President Roosevelt assisting in the completion of a reciprocity treaty with Cuba.)

From the *Journal* (Minneapolis)

THE AMERICAN HERCULES
(A Swiss tribute to President Roosevelt. After the assassination of President McKinley President Roosevelt took vigorous measures against Anarchists.)
From *Nebelspalter* (Zurich)

THE NEW BROTHERHOOD OF STRENUOSITY
(Apropos of the German Emperor's request as to his American yacht.)
From the *North American* (Philadelphia)

velt exactly as he had treated Mr. Hobart. Mr. McKinley had been true to this promise in so far as he had found opportunity.

Mr. Roosevelt, furthermore, was on terms of personal friendship with several members of Mr. McKinley's cabinet. In an article prepared at the request of the present writer, for the REVIEW OF REVIEWS, in 1896, Mr. Roosevelt had discussed the office of Vice-President, and had held that its incumbent should have close and harmonious relations with the President and the cabinet in order to preserve continuity of policy and of administrative work in case of his being called to the executive chair through the President's death.

Mr. Roosevelt, therefore, did not have to hesitate or take counsel in September, in order to decide precisely what his general course of action should be. Because he knew his own mind, he was able to give the country instant and welcome reassurance. The fact that he was devotedly loyal to Mr. McKinley and a supporter of the administration's

BRER LION AND BRER EAGLE

" I ain't gwineter peck yo' tail, Brer Lion," sez Brer Eagle, sezee; " but aen agin, I ain't gwineter gush 'bout yo'. Brer Lion he 'low dey kin git 'long fine on dat track."

(" He has never gushed over England; nevertheless, his admiration and respect for England are sincere." *Daily Chronicle* correspondent on President Roosevelt's Policy.)

From the *Westminster Budget*

THE NATION ENDORSES PRESIDENT ROOSE-
VELT'S COURSE
From the *Times* (Minneapolis)

THE WASHINGTON SCHOOLMASTER
From the *Chronicle* (Chicago)

policies, made it the easier for him to as-
sume his new responsibilities.

He immediately declared that it would be
his intention to carry out unbroken the
pending plans and policies of the administration in accordance with Mr. McKinley's
well-known views. He further invited every

ROOSEVELT'S BIGGEST GAME
From the *Herald* (New York)

ANOTHER DEMOCRATIC DISASTER

(President Roosevelt, by his anti-trust legislation and his settlement of the coal strike, has pulled out the main supports of the Democratic platform for the impending campaign.)—From *Judge*

member of Mr. McKinley's cabinet to retain his portfolio, with an earnestness that not one of them could withstand.

Almost at once in his administration he had to face the problem of enforcing the Sherman anti-trust law against railroad and industrial combinations. He took the safe position that it was his business to enforce the laws, and to follow the advice of the Attorney-General on the application of the law to any given case. This explains the action against the Northern Securities Company brought early in his administration by Attorney-General Knox.

In every subsequent case under that law, Mr. Roosevelt was not the crusader against modern business methods or aggregations of capital, but he was the firm executive, sworn to enforce the law, and acting always on the advice of his constitutional counselors, like Attorney-General Knox, and Secretary Root who was then at the head of the War Department.

Obviously, there were new policies to be shaped and executed relating to our

"WE SNATCHED THE CLOTHES OF THE WHIGS WHILE THEY WERE IN SWIMMING."— Disraeli.

(Referring to President Roosevelt's activity against the trusts, which the Democrats looked upon as being essential, according to Democratic doctrine.)

From the *Eagle* (Brooklyn, N. Y.)

THE NEW HERCULES
From *Nebelspalter* (Zurich)

(President Roosevelt begins to figure prominently in the foreign cartoons. In most of them he is well treated, although the Germans already show signs of treating him with that disfavor which they have visited of late upon all things American and English. In the drawing from *Kladderadatsch,* on this page, he stands at Uncle Sam's elbow while that old gentleman swaps stories with John Bull about their respective bad legs, labeled the Transvaal and the Philippines.)

UNCLE SAM : " I guess I can get ready for Thanksgiving now." *Inquirer* (Phil., November, 1902)

WHY NOT AN AUTOMATIC SUBSTITUTE?

" It is announced that the President will omit handshaking during his Western tour."

From the *Eagle* (Brooklyn, N. Y.)

JOHN BULL AND UNCLE SAM THE MOUNTAINCLIMBERS
From *Kladderadatsch* (Berlin)

THE HANDWRITING ON THE BAND WAGON
From the *Herald* (New York)

occupation of Cuba and our acquisition of
the Philippines and other insular possessions. But Secretary Root was in direct
charge of all these insular matters, as well
as of army reorganization; and Mr. Roosevelt, besides having profound respect for
Mr. Root's legal and executive talents, had
always been able to work with him in perfect harmony and co-operation.

Mr. Roosevelt's personality impressed
itself at once upon European statesmen and
the foreign press. His face became familiar
in the illustrated papers and cartoons of
Europe. He was frequently likened, in his
energetic and versatile qualities, to the German Emperor.

That distinguished monarch almost immediately, through diplomatic and less formal channels came into friendly touch with
the American President. He sent his
brother, Prince Henry, to visit this country
and to give his greetings to President
Roosevelt. The Emperor ordered an Amer-

" LOOK OUT, TEDDY ! "
From the *Times* (Denver)

ican yacht, and the President's daughter christened it at the launching in the presence of Prince Henry and Mr. Roosevelt.

.   The English press was cordial and appreciative, and felt that Roosevelt was a man of broad views of international affairs, while finding also some reassurance in his retention of Mr. John Hay as Secretary of State.

Even more sensational, at the time of it, than the prosecution of the Northern Securities Company, was the President's intervention in the great anthracite coal strike in Pennsylvania in 1902. The former case had involved a combination of three great Western railroad systems. The coal situation was the result of a stubborn contest between the organized miners who desired better pay, better conditions of labor, and the recognition of their union, and the five or six railroad corporations that had monopolized the anthracite coal production and were managing it for their own associated welfare.

The strike was so stubborn and complete that there was danger lest the great cities of New York and Philadelphia should be without their supply of fuel during the season of 1902-3, and general business interests were also suffering. The workmen desired to arbitrate, but the so-called coal barons refused, and stood upon their rights to manage their own affairs in their own way.

Mr. Roosevelt found that the law permitted him, through the Bureau of Labor, to make inquiry into all the facts and to seek to bring about conciliation. In the end he was able to secure a satisfactory arbitration, as a result of which the men were gainers; and the anthracite industry has been carried on in a peaceful way ever since.

The President's leadership in these matters had the approval of the country, and resulted in the election of a Republican Congress in the fall of 1902.

Furthermore, several State conventions, as for example those of the Pacific Coast, Iowa, Minnesota, Missouri, and others,—looking ahead two years,—made formal declaration of their intention to support Mr. Roosevelt for President in 1904.

PRESIDENT ROOSEVELT AS AN OPEN-AIR SPEAKER IN THE FALL OF 1902

CHAPTER XV
Asserting the Monroe Doctrine

THE VENEZUELA AFFAIR

THE POWERS (to President Roosevelt): "Would you mind caging yonder bird for me?"

From the *Pioneer Press* (St. Paul)

THE INTERNATIONAL ALPHONSE AND GASTON

ALPHONSE ROOSEVELT: "You arbitrate it, my dear Gaston."

From the *Journal* (Minneapolis)

TO ROOSEVELT

From *Tagarela* (Rio Janeiro)

(The above cartoon is from a weekly journal of politics and affairs published at Rio de Janeiro,—of course, in the Portuguese language,—called *Tagarela*. It is accompanied by a poem in four stanzas, which accuses the United States, under the tutelage of Roosevelt, of wishing to carry on further annexation. But this policy, it declares, has its dangers and anxieties; and while the "Monroe crowd" may push their policy by force in other directions, Brazil won't stand it,—"no, sir" (*nao senhor*)! "Why," says this Portuguese rhymster, "do you send your iron tub, which you call by the Indian name *Iowa?* If you propose to put your claws on Acre, you had better leave;" with more to the same effect.)

THE MONROE DOCTRINE
(A resounding word in the President's mouth.)
From *Nebelspalter* (Zurich)

OUR TURBULENT NEIGHBORS TO THE SOUTH

(Teddy no sooner turns his back than the children
begin to make trouble.)

From *Pasquino* (Turin)

THE ADOPTED CHILD

MR. ROOSEVELT: "It'll be some time before he's
fully developed, but I expect he'll be big enough
to help me in 1904 in the Presidential fight."

From the *Moon* (Toronto)

EARLY in 1903 several situations gave opportunity for the fresh declaration by Mr. Roosevelt of our interest in the affairs of the Latin-American republics, in accordance with the spirit of the Monroe Doctrine. The subjects of several European powers were in despair of being able to obtain compensation for claims due them from the government of Venezuela. A number of American citizens were in the same plight. A joint naval expedition was undertaken by Germany, France, and Holland to blockade Venezuelan coasts, seize ports and custom houses, and collect by force the sums considered by them to be due to their subjects.

Our government did not wish to see even a temporary occupation of South American soil by European governments on the pretext of collecting private debts. We were able to persuade President Castro on the one hand and the European powers on the other, to send representatives to Washington in order to ascertain what sums were fairly due under the claims. We then undertook to see that such claims as were allowed should in due time be paid. The position of our government made some sensation in Europe and a profound impression in South America.

Extra Session
Lesson
Panama Canal
Cuban Treaty

GUIDE TO THE ROCKY MOUNTAINS POWDER R. HOLE-IN-THE-WALL

THE TEACHER AND THE PUPILS

Roosevelt to the Senate: "Boys, this hurts me more than it does you."

(President Roosevelt, having made plans for a Western vacation tour, is anxiously awaiting the close of the Congressional session.)—From the *Inquirer* (Philadelphia)

Our general attitude toward Latin America was the more sharply observed, because at that time we were in the thick of negotiations preliminary to constructing the Trans-Isthmian Canal. The war with Spain had brought that long-dreamed-of project into the domain of actual possibilities. We had sent the battleship *Oregon* on a memorable voyage from the Pacific Coast around the continent of South America, to join our fleet in Cuban waters and strengthen it for the attack upon the Spanish squadron. We had realized the need of a canal for the sake of better protection of both coasts.

Furthermore, our new insular possessions in both oceans called for the Panama Canal as a logical sequel. A French company had obtained from the Republic of Colombia the necessary concession to dig a canal across the Isthmus of Panama. Many millions had been unwisely spent, great corruption and scandal had attended the history of the company in France, the enterprise had failed, and private capital was not available to resume it. Our American engineers for many years had preferred the Nicaragua route, and a private company had been formed which had made some beginnings. But the inevitable conclusion had been reached that no canal in the near future could be constructed, by

NO DISARMAMENT

(The "Big Stick" is needed for evils at home as
well as for possible use abroad.)

From the *Gazette-Times* (Pittsburg)

THE MASTER OF THE WORLD

POPE ROOSEVELT: "All that lies to the left of
this mark comes under the American political sphere
—and all on the right belongs to American trade."

From *Lustige Blätter*

COLUMBIA: "Pianissimo, Teddy!"

From the *Sun* (Baltimore)

PRESIDENT ROOSEVELT AND OLD EUROPE

From *Le Rire* (Paris)

either route, unless the United States Government should make a public enterprise of it and provide the necessary millions.

The country was almost unanimously prepared to proceed with the Nicaragua work when, by the efforts of the friends of the Panama scheme, a board of engineers was authorized to report upon the engineering and financial feasibility of both routes. It had been decided finally that Panama should be preferred if the assets of the French company could be bought for not more than $40,000,000. The next step was the drafting of a treaty with Colombia through Minister Herran and President Maroquin. Congress was called in special session to ratify this treaty, and also to pass upon the new constitution for the Republic of Cuba.

This constitution, with the significant part of which Secretary

A PRACTICAL FORESTER
(A subject that had attention all through Mr. Roosevelt's Presidency.)
From the *Pioneer Press* (St. Paul)

A GRIZZLY PATH: PRESIDENT ROOSEVELT AND THE TRUSTS
PRESIDENT ROOSEVELT: " Is it safe to shoot? "
THE BEAR: " Does he mean business? "
From the *Westminster Budget* (London)

THEODORE ROOSEVELT, PRESIDENT OF THE UNITED STATES
From *Kladderadatsch* (Berlin)

Root was identified, was one of the most important acts of statesmanship of all our recent history. It brought Cuba perpetually under our guaranty of internal order and financial responsibility.

The special session ended, Mr. Roosevelt was off for a Western trip, where in the Rocky Mountains he hunted the grizzly bear. He returned to a summer at Oyster Bay, where many questions of interest came before him, one of them being the endeavor to present to the Russian government the American view of the treatment of Jews in the Czar's dominions.

Another question of exceptional interest, relating also to our position on the North American continent, was the dispute with Canada regarding the Alaska boundary. This was settled by a tribunal, of an arbitral nature, composed of Americans on one side and Canadians and Englishmen on the other. It was a great triumph to have settled the Alaska boundary by amicable methods, and to have retained our unbroken coast-line as we had bought it from Russia.

ROOSEVELT AND THE CZAR.—A FRIENDLY EXCHANGE

"You cut up your Jews, I'll burn my negroes;" or, "Little presents preserve friendships."

From *Kladderadatsch* (Berlin)

ONE LITTLE MATCH MIGHT HAVE FIRED OFF THE WHOLE BUNCH

From the *Tribune* (Minneapolis)

VACATION DAYS AT OYSTER BAY

From the *Tribune* (Minneapolis)

SARGENT'S PORTRAIT OF PRESIDENT ROOSEVELT

(John S. Sargent, the eminent portrait painter, painted a picture of President Roosevelt in 1903, which met with favor at the White House and has remained there as the official portrait.)

CHAPTER XVI

Panama,—A New Sister Republic

ON TO PANAMA!
From the *Herald* (New York)

THE Congress of Colombia, sitting at Bogota, refused to ratify the treaty that its diplomatists had signed. It was in every way to the advantage of Colombia to have the United States dig the canal that the French company had abandoned. The treaty proposed that we should give Colombia ten million dollars for the privilege of conferring upon her a benefit of incalculable value. To have had us revert to the Nicaragua route would have been disadvantageous to Colombia for many centuries.

Furthermore, our return to the Nicaragua plan would have been ruinous to the people of the Isthmus of Panama, who were under no obligations whatsoever to the mercenary politicians at Bogota. Again, our choosing Nicaragua as the alternative would have made it impossible for the French company to have obtained its expected forty million dollars. Under these circumstances, the Isthmus of Panama declared itself an independent

THE MAN BEHIND THE EGG—From the *Times* (New York)

republic, all in the twinkling of an eye, with the substantial encouragement of the representatives of the French canal company, and with no unfriendliness or discouragement on the part of our government at Washington.

The few Colombian troops on the isthmus made no resistance.   American warships

THOSE LITTLE FELLOWS WANT TO LOOK OUT
WHEN I TOSS THE BALL

(Mr. Francis B. Loomis, who is here pictured as throwing the Medicine Ball of the "New Diplomacy," was Assistant Secretary of State at the time of the Panama revolution, and was very active in the negotiations having to do with that affair)—From the *Herald* (New York)

were prepared to keep order. The ten million
dollars that Bogota had refused was gladly

THE NEWS REACHES BOGOTA—From the *Herald* (New York)

accepted by the new Republic of Panama. The treaty was promptly signed that established our rights in the canal zone, and put the new republic virtually under our protection. The President of the United States was authorized by Congress to appoint a board of canal commissioners and to proceed with the work of construction. And all this constituted a notable episode in our history.

THE HUNTER HUNTED
From the *Herald* (Baltimore)

UNCLE SAM: "He's good enough for me."

(This striking cartoon by Homer Davenport was widely circulated in newspapers and on billboards and became the most prominent campaign document of the Republican party in 1904.)

From the *Evening Mail* (New York)

CHAPTER XVII
The Unanimous Endorsement of His Party

"DELIGHTED!"

(Senator Hanna, himself an aspirant for Presidential honors, reluctantly handing to President Roosevelt the endorsement of the Ohio convention.)—From the *Herald* (New York)

MR. ROOSEVELT had been having the sort of strenuous experiences as President that were in every way congenial to him, and the American public had undoubtedly approved of his policies and actions in most essential respects. It was not to be expected, however, that his renomination could come without opposition.

Senator Hanna, of Ohio, chairman of the National Republican Committee, and close friend of the late President McKinley, had become the most masterful personage in the Senate, not excepting Mr. Aldrich. Senator Hanna had broadened his interests. He espoused the cause of organized labor. He accounted himself responsible more than any one else for the practical steps that were making the Panama Canal a realized fact. In short, he was a candidate for the Presidency, and was effecting a powerful

'POSSUM OR CHICKEN?
(Capturing the colored vote!)
From the *Herald* (Baltimore)

TAKING THE BULL BY THE HORNS

(This cartoon refers to the action of the President in bringing suit against the Northern Securities Company.)

From the *Journal* (Minneapolis)

SOME TROUBLE WITH THE TARIFF TEAM

From the *Eagle* (Brooklyn, New York)

(Ohio, led by Hanna, had adopted a "stand-pat" high tariff platform, and Iowa had accepted Cummins' planks on reciprocity and revision.)

BLOCKING THE WAY

(Senator Aldrich's financial reforms in that session of 1902-3 were blocked by the mass of business in the House of Representatives.)

From the *Times* (Minneapolis)

UNCLE SAM'S NEED OF AN ELASTIC CURRENCY

PRESIDENT ROOSEVELT: "You see, those galluses ought to have rubber in them, so that when Uncle Sam stoops to move the sheaf there won't be much strain on the buttons."

From the *Pioneer Press* (St. Paul)

UNCLE SAM: "Now let's see you punch the bag."
From the *Herald* (New York)

organization of politicians throughout the country in his own behalf.

A good many States as early as 1902 had endorsed Roosevelt. The question arose whether the Ohio convention of 1903 would speak favorably of his administration. Mr. Roosevelt, who was hunting in the West, sent a famous message that resulted in Ohio's recognition of him in its platform. There was tariff agitation in the air, with Senator Hanna as the champion of the high-tariff "stand-pat" policy,—to use his own phrase,—while the Western leaders like Governor Cummins, of Iowa, were demanding revision. A great financial discussion was pending, moreover, having to do with the need of a different banking and currency system.

Mr. Roosevelt's tone was progressive, but his attitude was expectant rather than positive touching such questions. Those were matters for Congress rather than for the executive. But when serious scandals were current regarding the administration of the business of the postal system, Mr. Roosevelt was in no doubt as to his responsibility.

HE LAUGHS BEST WHO LAUGHS LAST

THE DEMOCRATIC DONKEY: "Ha, ha! the cat is out of the bag."
THE STRENUOUS REPUBLICAN BOY: "Yes, but it will soon be a dead cat."

From the *Journal* (Minneapolis)

THE FOREMAN GIVES ORDERS FOR RUSH WORK
From the *Times* (Minneapolis)

DRIVE THE KNIFE IN UP TO THE HILT!   From *Judge*, December 12, 1903

(President Roosevelt vigorously prosecuting corrupt corporations, as well as grafters and others, as
a result of the thorough investigation of the Postal frauds made by Fourth Assistant Postmaster-General
Bristow, who later became a United States Senator from Kansas.)

He took hold of the work of postal investigation with such vigor that he left no opportunity for the Democrats to make capital in the approaching campaign out of abuses which otherwise might have led to Republican defeat.

As the time for the choosing of delegates for the 1904 convention approached, the movement for Mr. Hanna's nomination disintegrated, partly because of the great strength of President Roosevelt with the people, and also partly because of the serious breakdown of Mr. Hanna's health. One after another of the great States, in their local conventions, instructed their delegates to support President Roosevelt. Ohio itself fell in with the general movement and sent a delegation instructed for the President.

The convention at Chicago turned out to be a great spontaneous demonstration in favor of the man who had acceptably served out three and a half years of Mr. McKinley's unexpired second term. If President McKinley had lived Vice-President Roosevelt would have been a candidate for the nomination in 1904. But he would not have been personally identified with the many stirring

ONLY COMPETENT NAVIGATORS NEED APPLY
From the *Post* (Cincinnati)

"A BIRD IN THE HAND IS WORTH TWO IN THE BUSH"
From the *Press* (Cleveland)

THE SNOW MAN AND THE HOT SUN
From the *Press* (Cleveland)

THE VALUE OF THE BINDER IN HARVEST-TIME

(Apropos of the pledging or "binding" of various State delegations to support Mr. Roosevelt in the nominating convention.)

From the *Brooklyn Eagle* (New York)

matters, both foreign and domestic, that had been crowded into the busy period from 1901 to 1904; and no one can make even a sagacious guess as to what would have happened. Senator Fairbanks, of Indiana, was nominated for Vice-President. Under other circumstances, Mr. Fairbanks would have been a formidable candidate for the Presidency. His friends had declared that he was the natural successor of Mr. McKinley, and that it had been Mr. McKinley's hope and wish, if he had lived, that Mr. Fairbanks should succeed him. But the bluff, powerful Hanna had intervened, and with the disintegration of the Roosevelt opposition which had centered around the chairman of the National Com-

SOME PROMINENT FEATURES OF THE CHICAGO CONVENTION
By Cartoonist Briggs, of the *American* (New York)

FRANK S. BLACK: "I come not to bury Cæsar, but to praise him."

(Gov. Black, who had been refused a second-term nomination for Governor in 1898, when Roosevelt took his place, made the nominating speech at Chicago in 1904.)

From the *World* (New York)

THE CHORUS OF ROOSEVELT HARMONY AT CHICAGO

From the *Post* (Cincinnati)

ROOSEVELT'S LAST INSTRUCTIONS TO THE REPUBLICAN ELEPHANT: "Whoop 'er up!"
From the *World* (New York)

mittee, it was quite impossible to rally around any other man's standard the various leaders and groups who did not like Roosevelt.

Mr. Root, Mr. Beveridge, ex-Governor Black, of New York, and others, made eloquent Roosevelt speeches in the convention, and there was incomparably more enthusiasm over Roosevelt's nomination in 1904 than there had been at Philadelphia over Mr. McKinley's renomination, or the placing of Roosevelt on the ticket as candidate for Vice-President. For years Roosevelt's friends had hoped to nominate him for the Presidency in the year 1904, and now they had actually accomplished their purpose.

THE CONVENTION HAS ARRIVED
From the *Herald* (New York)

CHAPTER XVIII
The Roosevelt-Parker Campaign

Stereograph copyright, 1904, by Underwood & Underwood New York

THE NOTIFICATION OF PRESIDENT ROOSEVELT AT OYSTER BAY IN 1904. (SPEAKER
CANNON STANDS ON THE PRESIDENT'S RIGHT.)

THERE was no well-defined issue in the campaign of 1904, as in the two previous
ones. In 1896 the question of sound money was threshed out and permanently
settled. In 1900 the people ratified the expansion policy, and the momentous national and international developments that followed our war with Spain. In 1904 the real
question was whether the people were well enough pleased with the man who had succeeded McKinley by a fateful accident to give him another four years' lease of power.

Wall Street interests were bitterly opposed to Mr. Roosevelt, because his investigation and prosecution of various trusts and corporations, and his attacks upon railroad rebates and like abuses had for the time being not only checked the prosperous schemes
of many promoters, but had also confused and disturbed legitimate business,—the whole
fabric of corporation finance and control being so closely interwoven. Thus Wall Street,
largely under Democratic leadership, had undertaken a more positive part in politics than
ever before. If only the Republicans could be prevented from nominating a man as bold

A VERY STOUT "STRING" TO IT

(Apropos of the struggle over the Cuban reciprocity
treaty.)

From the *Record* (Philadelphia)

ON COMMON GROUND

(President Roosevelt congratulates ex-President Cleveland
on the birth of a boy.)

From the *Ohio State Journal* (Columbus)

"Brummel" Roosevelt: "Ah! who is your fat friend?"

(Mr. Cleveland had made a speech at the Louisiana Purchase celebration at St. Louis, in 1903, and
it was thought at the time that he might possibly become a candidate for the Democratic nomination for
President and run against Roosevelt, who also attended the celebration.)

From the *Herald* (New York)

MR. ROOSEVELT: "This is so sudden."
From the *Tribune* (Chicago)

NOT A CLOUD IN SIGHT
(Except that made by the factory chimneys.)
From the *Inquirer* (Philadelphia)

and aloof as Roosevelt, and the Democrats could be persuaded to nominate a representative of their conservative wing rather than a radical like Bryan, Wall Street would have nothing to fear from the result of the election. So the "magnates" reasoned.

UNCLE SAM: "Never swap pilots while crossing a stream."—From the *North American* (Philadelphia)

Thus in 1903 and early in 1904 Wall Street had done its best to aid in the movement to secure the nomination of Senator Hanna in place of Mr. Roosevelt; and as early as 1903 certain eminent legal advisers of Wall Street had selected Judge Alton B. Parker (then chief justice of the highest court of the State of New York) as an excellent representative of the so-called " safe and sane " type of Democratic candidates. All this was in no way to Judge Parker's discredit; for he was an upright judge and a public man of sound views and a well-poised mind. Mr. Bryan had been twice defeated; and Judge Parker, though of a different school of political thought and training, had maintained his party regularity at all times, just as Roosevelt on his

SPIKED
(Judge Parker spiking the Republican campaign gun by his gold issue telegram to the St. Louis convention.)
From the *World* (New York)

side had been a Republican under all conditions.

Judge Parker was not widely known to the country, and his candidacy could not be otherwise than the merely negative one of opposition to Roosevelt. It was not possible for the Democrats to frame any successful issues. They could not ask boldly for tariff reform, because the South had become protectionist. They talked of scandals in administration, but the country knew that Roosevelt had cleaned out the Post Office frauds with as much vigor as any Democratic President could have

G. O. P.: "There's my man; where's yours?"
DEMOCRACY: "Oh, I'm waiting for an inspiration."
From the *Globe* (New York)

STRENUOUS VICE-PRESIDENTIAL CANDIDATE DAVIS AND WHAT A FRIEND CALLS
"A FEW OF HIS STUNTS."
From the *American* (New York)

shown. They could not denounce Roosevelt as a foe of trusts and corporations, because the major part of the Democratic party had always professed to be far more deeply opposed to monopoly and corporate aggrandizement than the Republicans.

In short, the logic of the situation was with Roosevelt. The people of the country, regardless of party, liked both the man and his policies. As the campaign progressed the Democratic managers denounced the Republicans as collecting large campaign funds from the very trusts and corporations that Mr. Roosevelt was supposed to be fighting. Moreover, Wall Street quickly lost confidence in itself as a political Warwick, and was inclined to disavow Judge Parker's candidacy as of its choosing. Doubtless various corporation interests contributed to both campaign funds; and it is unquestionably true that the greater part of the responsible business men of the country thought it better to keep Roosevelt and the Republicans in power than to bring in the Democrats on a dubious platform, with no knowledge of the make-up of a prospective Democratic cabinet.

Associated with Mr. Roosevelt was Secretary Hay, in charge of our foreign affairs; Mr. Root (who had just been succeeded by Mr. Taft), in charge of the War Depart-

PRESIDENT ROOSEVELT AS A PHRENOLOGIST

"It is difficult to find out from our opponents what are the real issues upon which they propose to wage this campaign."—Roosevelt's letter of acceptance.—From the *News* (Nashville)

INDORSED BY THE MAINE FARMERS

(Referring to the large Republican majority in the Maine election of 1904, which came before the general elections of November.)

From the *Evening Telegraph* (Philadelphia)

"WHAT IS ONE MAN'S MEAT IS ANOTHER MAN'S POISON"

(The cartoonist wishes to convey the idea that Roosevelt wants to talk and that Parker is quite happy to be silent.)

From the *News* (Baltimore)

ment and our island dependencies; Mr. Knox, brilliantly heading the judiciary department; and that remarkable campaigner, the Hon. Leslie M. Shaw, who had succeeded Mr. Gage as Secretary of the Treasury.

The President's Secretary, Mr. Cortelyou, had been secretary to President Cleveland, then to President McKinley; and three successive Presidents testified to his ability and faithfulness. He had political tact, administrative skill, and absolute honesty. He it was whom Mr. Roosevelt selected to conduct the campaign, and to serve as chairman of the National Republican Committee. One of the notable achievements of Mr. Roosevelt's first administration had been the creation of the new Department of Commerce and Labor, and Mr. Cortelyou had been promoted to the cabinet as Sec-

HOW TO MILK THE BEEF TRUST

(The Democrats regarded the Garfield report on the Beef Trust as very inoffensive, and found political reasons.)

From the *World* (New York)

The issue.—From the *World* (New York)   Two views of the President.—From the *Eagle* (Brooklyn)

TWO DEMOCRATIC CARTOONS ON THE "MILITARY" ROOSEVELT

THE TWO ROOSEVELTS

(The Roosevelt as real history will picture him—and—the Roosevelt as the demagogues now paint him.)

From *Judge*

retary of this new department. Mr. Roosevelt had advanced his assistant secretary, Mr. William Loeb, Jr., to succeed Mr. Cortelyou as Secretary to the President.

Of the bureaus grouped together under the Secretary of Commerce and Labor, the

THE ATTORNEY-GENERAL HAS A NEW JOB

KNOX: " Mr. Roosevelt, you'll have to get some-body else to tend to this pig, because Mr. Penn wants me to go to work for him."

From the *Journal* (Kansas City)

THE PRESIDENT (to Mr. Paul Morton, the new Secretary of the Navy): "You have done so well with the cars, now let's see what you can do with the ships."

From the *Leader* (Cleveland)

POPULIST CANDIDATE WATSON CHALLENGING THE OTHER PRESI-
DENTIAL CANDIDATES TO TALK

From the *Post* (Washington)

most important was a new one called the Bureau of Corporations. Mr. Roosevelt placed at the head of this bureau the Hon. James R. Garfield, transferring him from the post of Civil Service Commissioner. These are the names of a very few of the strong and able men with whom Mr. Roosevelt was surrounded. Mr. Hitchcock, of St. Louis, Secretary of the Interior, was exposing and prosecuting land frauds in the West, while the new Bureau of Corporations was investigating the Beef Trust, the Standard Oil Trust, and other corporations accused of violating the Sherman anti-trust law.

Under the circumstances, Mr. Roosevelt's overwhelming triumph at the polls was to have been expected. All sections of the country seemed to be contented with the outcome, and Judge Parker,

CONGRATULATIONS IN ORDER

ROOSEVELT: "De-e-lighted to hear that you have a cinch."

PARKER: "Allow me to congratulate you. I understand there is no longer any doubt but that you will be elected to the high office to which you aspire."

From the *Journal* (Minneapolis)

THE CALLING OF THE SECOND HAGUE PEACE
CONFERENCE

ROOSEVELT: "'Twill help to make the pot boil."

From the *Eagle* (Brooklyn, New York)

AS THE CAMPAIGN WAS ENDING

(Parker sits dejected at the foot of the Roosevelt pedestal.)

CÆSAR PLATT (to Brutus Odell): "Et tu, Brute?"
"This was the most unkindest cut of all:
For when the noble Cæsar saw him stab,
Ingratitude, more strong than traitors' arms,
Quite vanquish'd him: then burst his mighty heart;
And, in his mantle muffling up his face,
Even at the base of Pompey's statue,
Which all the while ran blood, great Cæsar fell."
From the *World* (New York)

HE'D SINK EITHER OF THEM

(Neither party, this year, wishes to run the risk of associating itself with the trusts.)
From the *North American* (Philadelphia)

THE GREAT TRIUMPH OF 1904
From the *Evening Star* (Washington)

though badly defeated, was regarded as having lost no important States which Roosevelt might not have carried against any possible Democratic nominee.

Mr. Roosevelt felt that his victory was not of a strictly partisan nature, and that the country was entitled to know in just what spirit he accepted it. On the night of his election, therefore, he issued a statement declaring that under no circumstances would he be a candidate or accept a nomination in 1908.

There was already much political talk to the effect that Mr. Roosevelt had merely been serving out Mr. McKinley's term, and that his acceptance of another nomination in 1908 would not be in violation of the tradition that limits an American President to two consecutive terms. His friends and his

AFTER THE AVALANCHE OF NOVEMBER 8 (1904).—From the *Post* (Washington)

ROPING THE PRESIDENTIAL STEER
From *Caras y Caretas* (Buenos Aires)

"HERE WE ARE AGAIN!"
(Apropos of Mr. Roosevelt's triumphant election and
subsequent visit to the world's fair at St. Louis.)
From the *World* (New York)

opponents alike had been thus looking forward to the next contest. Mr. Roosevelt won
the approval and renewed confidence of the country in the decisive announcement he made.
It was believed that with no ambition to secure another nomination, he could give the
more devoted and patriotic attention to the service of the whole people in his high office.

ROOSEVELT'S VICTORY
(A cartoon of the day after election)
UNCLE SAM: "Now we can get up steam again."
From the *North American* (Philadelphia)

AFTER THE BATTLE
UNCLE SAM: "I'm glad the election is over. I'll
sweep out and get to work."
From the *Times* (Washington)

ALWAYS INCISIVE, DECISIVE, AND PRECISE!
(Referring to Roosevelt's election night statement of 1904 renouncing a third term.)
From *Judge*

There was nothing more remarkable than the contented acquiescence of the Democratic press in the result. The people of the South showed their approval in many ways that could not be mistaken, and flooded Mr. Roosevelt with invitations to visit their respective States and cities. It had been the good fortune of Mr. McKinley, in a period of declining partisanship, to be regarded as the President of the whole country without regard to section or party; and this general good-will was transferred to Roosevelt even as the mantle of Elijah had in ancient time fallen upon the shoulders of his successor.

TAKING THE OATH OF OFFICE AT WASHINGTON ON MARCH 4, 1905

CHAPTER XIX

As Peace-Maker and World Figure

IT was in the summer of 1904,—his renomination secured and his election certain,— that Mr. Roosevelt began clearly to emerge in the mature sense as one of the great world figures of his day. The completion of the second McKinley (Roosevelt) term had secured the full establishment of the policy of expansion. Our navy had become strong and efficient under Mr. Roosevelt's guidance. The army had been thoroughly reorganized through Mr. Root's constructive statesmanship and his ability to win the approval of Congress for his policies. We were gaining renown through extirpation of yellow fever in Cuba and our success in sanitary measures at Panama.

The international prestige of the United States was enormously increased, and in the eyes of the world President Roosevelt was the man who typified the Twentieth Century America. He had, of course, followed in McKinley's footsteps in so far as he saw the path of duty leading in that direction. But it had been easy to work with Mr. McKinley's appointees, and Mr. Roosevelt had found no difficulty in holding to his pledge of September, 1901, that he would do his best to carry out Mr. McKinley's plans.

Now, however, the country had deliberately chosen him for its helmsman, and there could be no doubt of its mandate to go forward according to his own judgment. It was not necessary to wait for inauguration day in March. The new mandate took effect on

AVE THEODORE!

election day in November, and his message to Congress in December came with a strength and force that had perhaps been equalled in none of his previous state papers. It was then that he laid down that guiding principle of the " square deal,"—the determination to secure justice to all men to the best of his ability, to capitalist as well as to workman; to humble immigrant or Asiatic coolie as well as to the descendants of the Pilgrims or the Patroons.   And recognizing the commanding prestige that the United States had secured abroad as a result of its new policies and recent growth, the Roosevelt administration gladly accepted the responsibilities and the opportunities that go with prestige and power.

ALL HIS OWN

(Mr. Roosevelt, after completing President McKinley's second term, entered upon his own elective term of four years.)

CONGRESS OPENS

(The President hastening to the Capitol with voluminous proposals for new legislation.)

From the *Evening Herald* (Duluth)

THE NOBLEST ROMAN OF THEM ALL.—From *Judge* (New York)

The influence of the United States was henceforth to be exerted on behalf of international peace and good will. Our government promptly took the lead in proposing to the powers of Europe the holding of a second peace conference at The Hague, with a view to completing several steps that had been left for a future gathering by the original conference of 1899. The proposal met with general European favor, and Mr. Roosevelt was everywhere accorded the credit for initiating the gathering,—although our government very gracefully consented that Russia should issue the formal invitations, as for the original conference.

The breaking out of the fierce and regrettable war in Manchuria between Russia and Japan led to the postponement of the peace gathering until after that conflict had been

WHICH WAY?—From the *Record-Herald* (Chicago)
(He [the Senate] will make no mistake if he follows the footprints.)

BUT THE DOMINANT NOTE OF IT'S (AMERICA'S) HIGHEST CULTURE, ITS MOST PERSISTENT SPIRIT, HAS BEEN THAT RIGHTEOUSNESS WHICH EXALTETH A NATION, THAT OBEDIENCE TO THE INNER LIGHT WHICH LEADS ALONG THE PATHS OF PEACE"
SECRETARY HAY.

UNCLE SAM, ADVANCING WITH ROOSEVELT AND HAY TOWARD THE TEMPLE OF UNIVERSAL PEACE, INDORSES MR. HAY'S SENTIMENTS, AND ADDS : " And we'll continue right along the same path, boys ! "
From the *Ohio State Journal* (Columbus)

brought to an end, with its sharp, fresh lessons of the horrors of war and the need of preventing it by constant endeavor to substitute diplomacy, arbitration, or a permanent high court of justice among the nations. The proposal of a peace conference by so militant a personage as Mr. Roosevelt gave some of the cartoonists of this country, as well as of Europe, the opportunity for satire that was invoked rather in humor than in malice.

Mr. Roosevelt was everywhere mentioned as the man who was " bound to have peace even if he had to fight for it." The idea of the " Rough Rider " seeking to compel the angel of peace to exercise her gentle ministrations, made the world smile cheerfully and helped the good cause not a little.

The fact is that until the peace of the world is firmly established by universal treaties, and ample provision for international courts and international police, certain nations must take it upon themselves

DOUBTING THE ROUGH RIDER'S PEACEFUL PROPOSAL
THE GODDESS OF PEACE : " Fly away, my doves. Roosevelt would snare you."
From *Fischietto* (Turin)

LORD OF THE NEW WORLD
ROOSEVELT : " Take that statue of Frederick the Great away, until a statue of Monroe has been set up in Berlin."
(Referring to a statue presented to the United States by Emperor William.)
From *Der Floh* (Vienna)

PRESIDENT ROOSEVELT'S PROPOSAL TO HOLD A SECOND PEACE CONFERENCE AT THE HAGUE, AS IT SEEMS TO A GERMAN SATIRIST, WHO IS THINKING OF ALL THAT HAS HAPPENED SINCE THE CZAR CALLED THE FIRST CONFERENCE.

PRESIDENT: "Gentlemen, I thank you for coming; it is the best witness to the enthusiasm with which you have hitherto regarded the Czar's idea of a universal peace."
From *Ulk* (Berlin)

for the Pacific Ocean and the Farther East, we had also a duty to perform in that region. It was our business to maintain friendly relations with Japan and to help support the integrity of China. With Alaska, the Sandwich Islands, and the Philippines in our possession, besides our great States of the Pacific seaboard, and with the Panama Canal in process of construction, it was evident that our interests in the Pacific had become larger than those of any other single power.

Mr. Roosevelt's attitude was not belligerent, to use their own influence and power to help keep the world in order. Mr. Roosevelt saw this duty clearly, and had no shrinking from its performance. He did not in the least object to being pictured as the "World's Constable." He believed that it was quite clearly the business of the United States to maintain peace and order throughout the whole of North America and the regions around the Caribbean Sea, including the West Indies, Central America, and the countries on the northern coast of South America.

He regarded it as our duty, furthermore, through friendliness and good will, to serve the cause of peace for the remainder of South America. As

THE ANGEL OF PEACE: "Help! help!"
From the *World* (New York)

THE WORLD'S CONSTABLE
Judge, January 7, 1905

but, on the contrary, was most tactful, and friendly toward all the powers of America, Europe, and Asia. But it was an attitude of firmness and of conscious recognition of power. Instead of arousing the hostility of an ambitious monarch and empire like those of Germany, this American attitude helped to establish us in the good-will of the people and the government of that great nation. Further, we were more free from differ-ences of opinion with the people and government of the British Empire than at any previous time in all our history.

A certain masterfulness that the administration had assumed in its international relations was also felt in its policies of law enforcement at home. The question had been boldly asked whether the great aggregations of capital had not become so powerful as to be able to control politics, the press, and the organs of government. Mr. Roosevelt stood firmly on the ground that law and government must be supreme over the corporations created under the law. It was to be a long and difficult struggle,—that of finding the best way to regulate and control the forces of modern business without hampering them in their proper development and progress. It is by no means to be asserted that Mr. Roosevelt

CHORUS OF GRAFTERS AT THE WINDOW: "I wonder what he's going to say about us?"
From the *Tribune* (Chicago)

ROOSEVELT AS THE RISING SUN OF YANKEE
IMPERIALISM
(A Spanish view.)
From *Hojas Selectas* (Barcelona)

UNCLE SAM (to President Roosevelt) : "Before you
can bring about world peace, you must establish
peace in your own land by killing the trust monster."
From the *Amsterdammer* (Amsterdam)

possessed any rare or peculiar wisdom in his
dealing with such subjects.

He had no desire to destroy the forces of
modern business. He had none of the antagonism toward corporations that Mr.
Bryan had always shown. But he perceived

THE TWO DOVES OF PEACE
From the *World-Herald* (Omaha)

HE REJOICES OVER HIS LL.D. FROM
PENNSYLVANIA
DR. HOHENZOLLERN TO DR. ROOSEVELT : "While
we are in these togs, why not review my ships at
Kiel ? "
From the *Amsterdammer* (Amsterdam)

THE CHICAGO PIG STY
(Even the hogs blushed with shame when President Roosevelt revealed to them the hideous fate awaiting them at American stockyards.)
From *Simplicissimus* (Munich)

KINDRED SPIRITS OF THE STRENUOUS LIFE
(The German Kaiser and President Roosevelt.)
From *Punch* (London)

that if some great capitalistic enterprises were beneficent in their methods and results, others were guilty of oppression, and were prospering through disregard both of the laws of the land and of the natural rights of a host of citizens. Mr. Roosevelt tried, therefore, to find some workable applications of justice, with government and law supreme.

CONFISCATED BY THE BERLIN POLICE (See text on p. 128)
From *Punch* (London)

During the Presidential campaign, the trusts considered it talk for political effect.

At the present time, they think Roosevelt was really in earnest.

THE ILLEGAL TRUST IS BEGINNING TO WAKE UP TO AN UNPLEASANT FACT

From the *Tribune* (Chicago)

About some questions he was an opportunist. For example, he would person-

THE ROOSEVELT POLICY—PRESIDENT OF THE WHOLE COUNTRY

From the *Eagle* (Brooklyn)

A STRENUOUS PERFORMANCE

PROFESSOR ROOSEVELT (in his great trust act): "Ladies and gentlemen: In order to demonstrate the possibility of controlling these powerful creatures, not all of them equally tractable, I will now descend into their midst." (Proceeds to get out of his depth.)

From *Punch* (London)

ally have been glad to see a revision of the tariff undertaken somewhat early during his second administration. He did what he could to bring the question before Congress and the country. But he found that Congress was not ready for tariff revision, and that there was no compelling sentiment in favor of it anywhere in the country. His convictions on the tariff question were not of a sort that made him regard it as his duty to go forth upon a crusade against the Dingley tariff. As a party question and as a sectional question, the tariff was no longer in the thick of bitter controversy. It had become a business man's question and one of industrial evolution.

UNCLE JOE IN NO HURRY
(Tariff revision not greatly disturbing the Speaker
of the House.)
From the *Evening Mail* (New York)

PULL, THEODORE ! PULL !
(President Roosevelt and Chairman Cannon in the
tariff revision tug of war.)
From the *Record-Herald* (Chicago)

It was not only the prestige and the
power of the United States in world matters, but it was also the confidence felt in
President Roosevelt himself, and in the
fairness and good will of our government
and people, that made it possible for Mr.

Roosevelt, in the summer of 1905, to bring
about a conclusion of the war between Russia and Japan and a settlement of the is-

**OH, YES, THEY'RE PULLING TOGETHER ALL
RIGHT**
From the *Journal* (Minneapolis)

**THE PRESIDENT AND SECRETARY HITCH-
COCK ARE AFTER BIG GAME IN THE PUBLIC
LANDS OF THE NORTHWEST**
From the *Post* (Washington)

IN DOUBT

President Roosevelt: " I don't feel quite certain that I can separate those fellows with this branch."

From the *Borsszem Jankó* (Budapest)

CONGRATULATIONS

From the *North American* (Philadelphia)

sues involved by the adoption of a treaty of peace.

This was perhaps the crowning act of Mr. Roosevelt's career. Russia's misfortunes in the war made it highly desirable for her that hostilities should end. Japan's financial resources were becoming strained, and it was better for her future power and prestige to end the war promptly than to continue it. Both countries were on terms of especial friendship with the United

THE "BIG STICK" IN A NEW ROLE

Uncle Sam (looking at the olive branches wreathing the Roosevelt club): " Well, I guess a little strenuosity is worth while in peace as well as in war."

From the *Press* (Philadelphia)

THE END OF THE PEACE CONFERENCE

From *Klods-Haus* (Copenhagen)

THE PEACE-
MAKER

("Now, be
good, boys, and
throw your-
selves at the
feet of this
divinity.")

From *Hojas
Selectas*
(Barcelona)

States. And thus Mr. Roosevelt was able to bring them
into negotiation for settlement, and through his influence and earnest intercession
and efforts, the Treaty of
Portsmouth was drafted and
signed, and one of the great
wars of history brought to an
end.

This achievement was in-
deed appreciated in the United
States as constituting a bright
page in the country's history.
But it was even more widely
recognized in Europe and

AT THE PEACE AGENCY

WITBOI : " Would you be good enough
to bring about peace between myself
and Trotha? I would likewise agree to
pay no war indemnifications whatever."

(The above refers to the uprising of
the Bauzelswarts under their chief,
Witboi, in German East Africa. This
uprising was finally suppressed by von
Trotha, then in charge of the military
affairs of the colony. The sign reads :
" *Great International Peace Agency*.
Orders carefully and promptly executed. Medals, diplomas and testimonials
from several Crowned Heads of Europe.")

From *Ulk* (Berlin)

THE TABLETS OF AZIT-TIGLETH-MĪPHANSI, THE SCRIBE.

NINETEENTH FRAGMENT.

In the lines numbered from 1 to 47, inclusive, accompanying the above " Tablet " of " Azit-Tigleth-Miphansi, the Scribe," published in London *Punch*, is recorded the situation of the belligerent forces of Russia and Japan just previous to the making of peace. " The Bit-Jappis, the heroes of Nippon," had played Jiu-Jitsu with the Russian armies—" with their *miriadz-ov-kossaks* in *moth-iten-kaftans*," and had them " all stymied and *bun-kahd*, checkmated and flummoxed." The Russian commander, meanwhile, " inspired by a passion for fighting . . . on paper, sits and twirls his *mustashiz* (mendaciously martial), writes fire-eating dispatches describing the pitiful state of Kuroki! Tells his poor little master, who *crouches-in-ermin*, that all is now ready—one word will let loose his victorious legions "; and that he " proposes to take for his breakfast next morning Oyama-on-toast, with Oku, and Nogi and Nodzu for luncheon, . . . that he can't quite decide which quarter of Tokio he'll live in." The chronicle goes on as follows :

48. Then did Teddy the Toothful, the lord of
49. the Yankiz, the king of the Cowboys,
50. the ruler of Hennessy, Dooley and
51. others,—a wonderful blend, Hohenzollern—
52. cum-Cody,—who dwells in the White House,
53. exchange his rough-riding, *vaquerolaik*
54. garments for a more or less accurate
55. classical costume with property wings
56. safety-pinned to his shoulders,—a sweeter
57. presentment of Peace one can hardly
58. imagine, . . . adjusting
59. his *pinzneh*, his face wreathing in smiles that
60. would easily reach from New York to Vancouver
61. his prominent teeth fairly gleaming with *hai-laitz*,
62. with the olive-branch sweetly extended
63. in nice little portly and spatulate fingers

64. and pointing his toes in a dancing position
65. he advanced to the parties concerned and,—
66. well, really, they *couldn't* resist him.
67. To the bay of the oyster did they come. . . .
68. The Bit-Jappis Komura did send
69. *sedéit, maikroskopik*, frock-coated and silent
70. and like as the shell of the oyster were his lips
71. closed and the pushing reporter could get no ad-
     mittance
72. and wore out his boots and his language together
73. as he tramped the *piyazza*.
74. But Nikkithetsar sent the doughty Dewitte
75. (they expected some muskovaithaîl and they
76. got it) ; with a *makhia-vclyan* keutniss selected
77. an *honest* diplomatist (no doubt of malice
78. aforethought)   E. T. R.

PRESIDENT ROOSEVELT, THE PEACE SHOWMAN
"Here, ladies and gentlemen, is the newest attraction. This bear, a ravenous beast of prey subdued by Togo and Oyama, is now so tame that he subscribes to anything that is dictated to him." From *Humoristische Blätter* (Vienna)

Asia, where the magnitude of the war and the profound consequences of an unforeseen kind that follow in the wake of so colossal a struggle were more vividly felt and better understood.

Thus, Mr. Roosevelt's international reputation as a peacemaker suddenly flamed up and filled the eyes of an astonished world. Congratulations came from all lands. The Emperor William of Germany is reported to have cabled: "The whole of mankind must unite in thanking you for the great boon you have given it." The cartoonists began with increasing frequency to picture Roosevelt and the German Kaiser together as "kindred spirits of the strenuous life"; and a cartoon in the London *Punch* to that effect was confiscated by the Berlin police as lacking in the reverence due to two men so noble and majestic, whereupon the irreverent car-

THE LATEST ECLIPSE
From the *World* (New York)

THE MAN OF THE HOUR
(The Cuban people congratulate President Roosevelt on his success as a peacemaker.)
From *La Discusion* (Havana)

He attends to San Domingo

He hands Mr. Castro a few

He jumps on the Senate

He writes on the race question

He lands on the Standard Oil Co.

He attends a banquet in New York

He superintends the preparations
for inauguration day

He passes a hot message to the
Senate

He pauses a moment to make
plans for a hunting trip

ONE OF MR. ROOSEVELT'S QUIET DAYS

From a cartoon by McCutcheon, of the Chicago *Daily Tribune*

THE PRESIDENT ON HIS PORCH AT OYSTER BAY
From a photograph taken in 1905

toonist, Mr. E. T. Reed, drew a caricature of his original cartoon. Both pictures are re-produced on page 122; and another amusing drawing by the same artist, which we have reproduced on page 127, records the deeds of the peace-making Theodore under the guise of an old Assyrian tablet and chronicle.

And thus the press of all Europe made much of the Treaty of Portsmouth; while the Norwegian parliament, at the first opportunity, awarded to Mr. Roosevelt the Nobel Prize as the man who had done the most within the year to promote the world's peace.

CHAPTER XX

The "Big Stick" at Home and Abroad

SOME casual remark of Mr. Roosevelt's, quoting the old proverb that it is well to speak softly but carry a big stick, had caught the visualizing imagination of the cartoonists; and on many occasions they have found it convenient to depict him as armed with a heavy club. He was not, however, making belligerent use of that or of other offensive implements in the year that followed his inauguration. There were many other matters of international concern in the spring and summer of 1905 besides the Russo-Japanese war and its termination. There was a Pan-American Con-

THE SENATE TO THE PRESIDENT: "Say! What's it about?"—From the *Herald* (Boston)

(Referring to Mr. Roosevelt's efforts to straighten out the finances of San Domingo.)

THE BIG STICK IN THE CARIBBEAN SEA
From the *Herald* (New York)

PRESIDENT ROOSEVELT (on his way to Texas): "Oh, things will be all right in Washington. I have left Taft sitting on the lid keeping down the Santo Domingo matter."—From the *Plain Dealer* (Cleveland)

THE ARRIVAL OF ROOSEVELT
(How the Texas bears had warning that somebody was coming.)
From the *Herald* (Rochester)

"THE CALL OF THE WILD"
(The wild animals which Mr. Roosevelt encounters on his hunting trip also prefer arbitration to war.)
From the *Eagle* (Brooklyn, New York)

THE PRESIDENT GOES A-HUNTING—LEADING THE SIMPLE LIFE IN COLORADO
From the *North American* (Philadelphia)

"THE WINNING OF THE WEST"
(Apropos of the reception tendered to President Roosevelt by the leading Democratic club of Chicago.)

From the *World* (New York)

gress at Rio de Janeiro, and we were bent upon using that occasion as a means of increasing our friendly relations with South America. Secretary Hay had passed away, and his place at the head of the Department of State had been filled by the Hon. Elihu Root.

Mr. Root, after five years of eminent service under McKinley and Roosevelt as Secretary of War, had returned to the practice of law in New York, refusing to be a candidate for governor and a prospective candidate for the Presidency in 1908, and having no ambitions for further public office. But the call to be Secretary of State is one that it has been the tradition of eminent New York lawyers to accept. Even while Secretary of War, Mr. Root had been the leading member of the cabinet, and the President's chief adviser in foreign matters involving legal knowledge. He brought to the post of

PRESIDENT ROOSEVELT'S FORTHCOMING FEAST,—A SOUTH AMERICAN VIEW OF THE LATEST APPLICATIONS OF THE MONROE DOCTRINE—From *Succesos* (Valparaiso, Chile)

Secretary of State a peculiar personal fitness for its duties, and a comprehensive knowledge of its problems.

Mr. Root, more than any one else, had devised the arrangement which brings Cuba under our protection and control in certain emergencies. It now devolved upon him to find a way for the regulation of the broken-down finances of the little republic of San Domingo. The European powers were bent upon a forcible collection of their debts, San Domingo having defaulted upon its foreign bonds. Our government virtually guaranteed a new issue of San Domingo securities, and was permitted to take charge of the custom-houses in order to satisfy foreign creditors and promote the peace of the distracted island. Mr. Root, mean-

PEACEMAKER ROOSEVELT: "I've mended worse rips."
From the *Star-Journal* (Pueblo)

MORE TROUBLE FOR THE INTERNATIONAL POLICEMAN
From the *Record* (Philadelphia)

THE YANKEE PERIL, AS PICTURED BY ONE
ARGENTINE JOURNAL

From *Caras y Caretas* (Buenos Aires)

ROOSEVELT AND ROOT IN BRAZILIAN EYES

(The *Malho*, of Rio Janeiro, commenting on a minor incident growing out of local political animosities in Argentine, reports the following alleged conversation between President Roosevelt and the Secretary of State: Roosevelt: "How is it, Brazil gave you flowers and her neighbor nation stones?" Root (calmly): "Each one gives what he has, Mr. President.")

Mr. Root's visit to South America was the chief topic of the cartoonists among our Latin neighbors to the south at the time.

From *Puck.*   Copyright 1904.   By permission.

WHAT WOULD LINCOLN DO?

(President Roosevelt, in dealing with matters of grave importance, was often guided by the thought of what Lincoln would do under the circumstances.)

THE STORY OF KETTLE HILL
(President Roosevelt entertaining the Japanese Peace
Commissioners at Oyster Bay.)
From the *Herald* (New York)

WHAT IT MAY COME TO
(Peace Missionary Roosevelt in a new *rôle*.)
From the *Journal* (Minneapolis)

while, proceeded upon a South American tour, visiting the Pan-American conference at
Rio and receiving tributes at the leading capitals of other South American republics.
    He had visited Canada with fruitful results for the settlement of all outstanding ques-
tions between the United States and the Dominion. His visit to South America was of
so tactful and sympathetic a character, and so appreciative of everything creditable in
South American statesmanship and progress, that it removed not a little of the prejudice
that had existed among the polite peoples of Latinic origin in the Southern republics

MARCHING THROUGH GEORGIA
(Referring to President Roosevelt's trip through some
Southern States in 1905.)
From the *Tribune* (Chicago)

REJOICING OVER THE END OF THE HUNT
THE BEARS : "We're glad he's gone."
From the *Tribune* (Minneapolis)

THE FIGHT OF HIS LIFE

(Roosevelt beginning his great fight for railroad regulation.)

From the *Eagle* (Brooklyn, New York)

THE PRESIDENT'S DETERMINATION TO HAVE RATE REGULATION CAUSES WORRY TO THE RAILROAD MAGNATES

From the *Leader* (Cleveland)

against what they regarded as the brusque, commercial Yankee nation.

Mr. Taft, furthermore, had come home

CHRISTMAS AT THE WHITE HOUSE—From *Judge* (New York)

(On his hobby, anti-railroad rebate laws.)

THE PRESIDENT AND THE HOSPITABLE SOUTH

(Some cartoons on this and the following page refer to one of Mr. Roosevelt's Southern trips.)

From the *Post* (Washington)

**PRESIDENT ROOSEVELT BEING WELCOMED
TO DIXIE LAND**

From the *Post* (Washington)

**PRESIDENT ROOSEVELT HOUSECLEANING
AGAIN**

(Apropos of a scandal in connection with the leak
of a government cotton report.)

From the *Constitution* (Atlanta)

UNDER THE PALMETTO TREE

THE SOLID SOUTH: "Well, sah, Cunnel Roosevelt, you all suttinly has powahful persuadin' ways. I keeps fohgettin' you ah a Republican, but I reckon you ah a Democrat on your mother's side."

From the *Tribune* (Chicago)

from the Philippines to take Mr. Root's former place as Secretary of War, and he had at once assumed a very influential place in the cabinet. With Mr. Root on his travels, and President Roosevelt in the West on a brief hunting trip, Mr. Taft was in special charge of the unfinished business relating to San Domingo, Cuba, and our outlying responsibilities in general. It was a little later on that a situation of chaotic turmoil somehow arose among the little republics of Central America. Again the man with the "Big Stick" spoke softly, and peace was restored. It was largely by Mr. Root's efforts that a plan was devised for settling Central American difficulties through a representative tribunal that was expected to prevent future hostilities among half a dozen small sovereignties. The plan was good, even if it has not as yet produced the expected results.

As the autumn advanced, the attention of the man who carried the big stick was centered upon the approaching session of Congress. It was his determination to secure the passage of a law that would put an end to the almost universal practice among the

THE SQUARE DEAL

From the *Spokesman-Review* (Spokane)

THEY HAVE TURNED THEIR MUD BATTERIES
AGAINST HIM

(President Roosevelt's vigorous fight against
wrongdoing of various kinds brought upon him all
sorts of abuse and calumny from these sources.)

From the *Spokesman-Review* (Spokane)

railroads of granting rebates to the large
corporations, and other favored shippers.
The principle of national regulation of rail-
roads had become firmly established, and it was considered that the one point above all
others most necessary to be secured was the equal and impartial treatment of all whose
business required them to use the means of interstate transportation. It was a hard
fight, but the legislation was secured, its results were accepted by the railroads, and a
great reform was put into effect that the railroads have since regarded as even more val-

A NEW TASK FOR THE ROUGH RIDER

(In the spring of 1906 a threatened coal strike en-
gaged the attention of the President.)

From the *Leader* (Cleveland)

"CAUGHT IN THE ACT"

(President Roosevelt turning the flashlight of the
Garfield report on the Standard Oil monopoly.)

From the *Press* (Philadelphia)

THE PARTIES AND THE PRESIDENT'S RAIL-
ROAD POLICY
From the *Post* (Washington, D. C.)

TRYING TO BLOCK HIS WAY
From the *Tribune* (Minneapolis)

uable to them than to those who had so strenuously fought against the rebate system.

Along with the granting of freight rebates, there disappeared the granting of free passes to politicians and their henchmen, which had been an abuse of almost incred-

UNCLE SAM (to the railroad trusts and obstruc-
tionists): "Give the President a chance."

From the *Evening Mail* (New York)

UNCLE SAM IS ON

SENATE: "Hey, Uncle, come quick. Look, see what the terrible Teddy has done now—Panama—silver coinage—Santo Domingan treaty—awful—wow!!!"

UNCLE SAM: "Say, I'm not half so much interested in what Teddy has done as in what you are not doing."

From the *Journal* (Minneapolis)

THE ROUGH RIDER: "San Juan Hill is not in it
with this brute."

From *Collier's Weekly*

THE THREE R'S
(President Roosevelt will impress them upon the
pupils of the Congress School.)

From the *Journal* (Minneapolis)

ible dimensions, and which had played no small part in the corruption of legislatures and the obstruction of honest government.

Mr. Roosevelt's messages to Congress for that period are elaborate discussions of the economic and social conditions of the country. Their value as presentments of fact, and as contemporary discussion of evils and remedies, will have great appreciation at the hands of the future historian. Thus in the message of December, 1906, statements are made regarding the working of the recent Railway Rate bill; and it is shown that this and other recent legislative steps toward the better regulation of interstate commerce had already been justified in experience. In view of conditions that led, in 1910, to the enactment of the new Railroad Rate bill, with its enlargement of the powers of the Interstate Commerce Commission, it is worth while to quote a little from Mr. Roosevelt's message of 1906. Let us take, for example, the following paragraphs:

It must not be supposed, however, that with the passage of these laws it will be possible to stop progress along the line of increasing the power of the national government over the use of capital in interstate commerce. For example, there will ultimately be need of enlarging the powers of the Interstate Commerce Commission along several different lines, so as to give it a larger and more efficient control over the railroads.

"JIU-JITSUED"
From the *Post* (Cincinnati)

HIS FAVORITE AUTHOR.—From the *Chronicle* (Chicago)

THE LEGISLATIVE SIDEWALK SNOWBOUND
The President's Message: "Get busy!"—From the *Journal* (Minneapolis)

It cannot too often be repeated that experience has conclusively shown the impossibility of securing by the actions of nearly half a hundred different State legislatures anything but ineffective chaos in the way of dealing with the great corporations which do not operate exclusively within the limits of any one State. In some method, whether by a national license law or in other fashion, we must exercise, and that at an early date, a far more complete control than at present over these great corporations,— a control that will, among other things, prevent the evils of excessive overcapitalization,—and that will compel the disclosure by each big corporation of its stockholders and of its properties and business, whether owned directly or through subsidiary or affiliated corporations.

These paragraphs set forth a program that Mr. Roosevelt well understood could not be carried out at once. It is precisely the program that President Taft took up in 1909, and that was included in (1) the Railroad Rate bill, which became a law in June, 1910; (2) the work outlined by President Taft for a commission to report upon the best way to regulate the issue of railroad stocks and bonds, and (3) the bill of Attorney-General Wickersham, providing for the federal incorporation of railroads and large industrial companies.

Many of the progressive ideas advocated by Mr. Roosevelt in 1905, and the two fol-

THE SPIRIT OF 1906

(With President Roosevelt, Speaker Cannon, and Senator Tillman marching in harmony, the national spirit of 1776 is recalled.)

From the *Herald* (New York)

THE LATEST RECRUIT

From the *Press* (Philadelphia)

"YOU'RE ANOTHER!"

From the *Journal* (Minneapolis)

"NEXT!"

From the *Plain Dealer* (Cleveland)

lowing years, which brought upon him the enmity and violent criticism of the exponents of great corporate wealth, had already, by the time Congress adjourned in the summer of 1910, found acceptance as self-evident and commonplace doctrine in the platforms of both wings of both great parties.

A NAUSEATING JOB, BUT IT MUST BE DONE

(President Roosevelt takes hold of the investigating muck-rake himself in the packing-house scandal.)

From the *Saturday Globe* (Utica)

CHAPTER XXI

Some Activities of a Versatile President

FOLLOW YOUR LEADER, THE NEW REPUBLICAN GAME
From the *Herald* (Salt Lake)

THE CANDIDATE
From the *Leader* (Cleveland)

"DEE-LIGHTED"
From the *Inquirer* (Philadelphia)

Stereograph, Copyrighted, 1906, by Underwood & Underwood N. Y.

PRESIDENT ROOSEVELT AT PANAMA RESPONDING TO THE WELCOME OF PRESIDENT
AMADOR

PRESIDENT ROOSEVELT'S hold upon the confidence of the country was again put to the test in the Congressional elections of 1906. It was recognized that the President and his policies formed the issue, and a clever cartoonist at the time depicted Mr. Roosevelt as the candidate in front of the polling booths of every State. The campaign was also notable as one in which the Republican party tried to obtain its funds by small popular subscriptions rather than in large sums from business interests.

Ever since the Civil War, the Republican party had made the protective tariff its shibboleth, and had relied upon the manufacturing interests to provide its election funds. This practise of collecting from wealthy business interests had been continued; but it became embarrassing when the government was attempting to enforce the Sherman anti-trust law to break up illegal railroad practices and dissolve industrial combinations.

The election having resulted in an emphatic endorsement of the administration, Mr. Roosevelt broke the traditions which had held our President strictly upon American soil by making a trip to Panama to inspect personally the sanitary and engineering work of our new Canal Zone, and to pay his respects to the young Republic of Panama, which he had been accused of creating. He came back prepared to refute the attacks that had been made upon our beginnings with the canal, and besides his regular message to Congress, at its assembling in December, he prepared a special message on conditions at Panama,

INSPECTING THE DITCH

Peace hath her trenches no less than——

From the *Inquirer* (Philadelphia)

NOW WATCH THE DIRT FLY!

From the *Globe* (New York)

"DEE-LIGHTED"

(President Roosevelt has illustrated his message to Congress. The American cartoonist welcomes him to the craft. No trouble finding something "to do with ex-president Roosevelt.")

From the *Journal* (Minneapolis)

providing each Congressman with a copy elaborately supplied with photographic illustrations.

Incidentally it may be said that these messages to Congress were much commented upon by reason of their use of the simplified spelling that had been recommended by a group of learned gentlemen who had banded themselves together to reform the spelling of the English language. They had appealed to Mr. Roosevelt during his summer vacation at Oyster Bay by telling him they had hit upon a method of arousing an apathetic nation to the adoption of phonetic spelling not by gradual process but by a sudden stroke. If Mr. Roosevelt would but use the simplified form himself, and instruct the Government Printing Office at Washington to put all public documents in this new phonetic dress, the reformed system would be virtually established, and the newspapers and public schools would have to follow.

A FEW SHOTS AT THE KING'S ENGLISH

"What Mr. Roosevelt means is to scrap the English language. He is a patriot, not a pottering Philologist," according to the London *Saturday Review*.

From *Collier's Weekly* (New York)

TWISTING THE LION'S TONGUE

FATHER TIME (closely examining small incision in tree-trunk): "Who's been trying to cut this tree down?"

"TEDDY" ROOSEVELT (in manner of young George Washington): "Father! I kannot tel a li.. I did it with my litl ax."

FATHER TIME: "Ah, well! Boys will be boys!"

From *Punch* (London)

KIKT OUT!

From the *Spokesman-Review* (Spokane)

THE NEW SCHOOL
From the *Plain Dealer* (Cleveland)

The outcome proved, however, that there were some things that even the dauntless President could not accomplish. The English language resisted the attack. Mr. Roosevelt accepted his defeat with entire cheerfulness. There was little if any reformed spelling in his Romanes lecture at Oxford three or four years later. About spelling reform,

TEACHING THE YOUNG IDEA HOW TO SPELL
From the *World* (New York)

THIS DOES SETTLE IT
(President Roosevelt positively cannot accept the nomination for a third term; he has undertaken the introduction of spelling reform, and that is trouble enough for one man.)
From the *Tribune* (Minneapolis)

THE PRESIDENT CROWNED AGAIN

From the *World* (New York)

THE ANGEL OF PEACE

(The Germans think he looks uncommonly like the American President. But they don't quite like his looks for all that.)

From *Kladderadatsch* (Berlin)

as about the revision of the tariff, Mr. Roosevelt was, in fact, at heart an opportunist. At one time or another he urged both reforms at the request of his earnest

MR. ROOSEVELT TO NORWAY: "Delighted!!" (The award of the Nobel peace prize.)

From the *Press* (Philadelphia)

"WAIT JUST A MOMENT, MR. PRESIDENT"

From the *Leader* (Cleveland)

and convinced friends; but he himself could afford to abide the general verdict and await the slower processes of time.

Through all this period there was constant and relentless effort in the Department of Commerce and Labor, the Department of the Interior, and the Department of Justice to prove and to punish violations of law by great corporations. Mr. Hitchcock had retired from the Interior Department, to be succeeded by Mr. James R. Garfield. Mr. Cortelyou, after the successful campaign of 1904, had become Postmaster-General, and in the middle of Mr. Roosevelt's second term he had been transferred to the head of the Treasury Department upon the retirement of the Hon. Leslie M. Shaw. Mr. Moody, who had succeeded Mr. Knox as Attorney-General (Mr. Knox having entered the Senate) was as energetic as Knox himself in the prosecution of offending corporations. Meanwhile, a vacancy having occurred on the Supreme Bench, Mr. Moody was appointed to that high tribunal, and Mr. Charles J. Bonaparte became Attorney-General.

"TEDDY THE GOOD" IN A NEW ROLE

" It is a very laudable purpose, but would anybody but Theodore Roosevelt ever think of dedicating a Christmas windfall of $40,000 for such a purpose?"

From the *Times* (Brooklyn)

UNCLE SAM (to the President): " Here, Theodore, drop that and get back to your old job."

From the *Blade* (Toledo)

JOHN BULL: " Thank you, Mr. Roosevelt, for the prompt kindness of your navy and your people in this terrible disaster at Jamaica!

From the *Westminster Gazette* (London)

A BUSY DAY IN THE CABINET
From the *Tribune* (Chicago)

"I TAKE MY PEN IN HAND"
From the *Evening Mail* (New York)

ALL READY FOR THE FIREWORKS
From the *Tribune* (Chicago)

Mr. Oscar S. Straus had succeeded Mr. Cortelyou as head of the Department of Commerce, and Herbert Knox Smith had become head of the Bureau of Corporations succeeding Mr. Garfield. Mr. Pinchot, who had for a long time been Chief Forester under the veteran head of the Department of Agriculture (Mr. Wilson), had by this time become an official of great influence and power.

THE PRESIDENT AND THE UNITED STATES SENATE
(The hen vociferously protests, but Farmer Roosevelt selects the eggs just the same.)
From the *Saturday Globe* (Utica)

PRESIDENT ROOSEVELT AS SENATOR RAYNER
SEES HIM
From the *Globe* (New York)

the law was enforced against oppressive combinations.

A delicate situation, moreover, had arisen on account of anti-Japanese riots in Pacific Coast States. Japanese laborers were not excluded under the law that prevented Chinese immigration. A good many Japanese laborers were finding employment. California demanded the extension of the Exclusion act to Japanese and Korean laborers. Japan's victory in the great war against Russia had naturally enhanced the consciousness of power and importance among the Japanese people, and they resented the idea of exclusion from America. The situation was met with tact and good-will by both governments.

The great financial panic that spread from the banks and trust companies of New York City throughout the country in the last weeks of 1907 created situations that called

His strength was due to the greatness of the situations he had to deal with, and the breadth of his view and the strength of his grasp. When Mr. Pinchot had taken office years before, we were practically without forest reserves. No one had supposed that our timber supply could be exhausted. But by degrees it came to be understood that great lumber companies were managing to monopolize the forest areas that remained as part of the Western public domain, and that for reasons of large public policy the remaining timber areas must be kept as national forests.

President Cleveland had made an important beginning in this direction; President McKinley had gone still further, and it remained for President Roosevelt, with his exceptional knowledge of the physical conditions of the country, to make forest preservation, and the protection of other great natural resources, one of the leading concerns of his administration. There was earnest co-operation among all the executive departments to protect the public domain, to enforce the Interstate Commerce law in the interest of the people, and to see that

THE TRUTH ABOUT THE PANIC

"Teddy, in the heat of his eloquence, beating the table, caused to fall a number of banks, which were already worm-eaten. Seizing the advantage of this accident, he began to thunder against business corruption. Yet, during nearly eight years of his 'reign' he did nothing to suppress these corrupt practices. He escaped at the end of his term by stirring up a great scandal.

"Teddy, you fool nobody. We all know that your anger is put on to assure you a fine wind-up."

From *Figaro* (Vienna)

NO MOLLY-CODDLING HERE

(This is the prevailing Wall Street notion of President Roosevelt's attitude toward corporate interests.)

From the *Globe* (New York)

WALL STREET PAINTS A PICTURE OF THE PRESIDENT

From *Collier's Weekly* (New York)

for government relief. Mr. Roosevelt, through his Secretary of the Treasury, Mr. Cortelyou, acted with his accustomed promptness. The money stringency was relieved by the government's proposal to issue and place on the market many millions in Panama Canal bonds, and many more millions in short-term notes under a law that had been enacted in the period of the Spanish War.

The panic illustrated the need of a reform in our money and banking system; and Mr. Roosevelt did everything in his power to promote the view of those who were working for banking reform and an elastic currency. There were many financiers embarrassed by the panic who imagined at the time that President Roosevelt's efforts to enforce the law as respects interstate commerce and industrial monopolies had created distrust and brought about the crisis that was so disastrous to the stock market. Most of those men, two years later, in looking back upon the course of events, would have acknowledged their entire mistake as to the facts and causes.

The panic had been brought about by conditions of over-speculation and bad business methods that were brought clearly to light when the strain came. The panic, in other words, was but a symptom of those very

THE RAILROADS AND ROOSEVELT
(Before and after the long struggle for anti-rebate legislation.)

From the *Evening Star* (Washington)

" WHOA ! "

(Apropos of the President's order reserving the public timber and coal lands.)

From the *Record-Herald* (Chicago)

THE THUNDERER

Cæum ipsum petimus stultitia neque,
Per nostrum patimur scleus,
Iracunda Jovem ponere fulmina.
—*Horace, Ode III*, 38-40.

From *Collier's Weekly* (New York)

evils in the industrial and commercial world that Mr. Roosevelt had been pointing out and trying to remedy.

NO OCCASION FOR GENERAL ALARM

PRESIDENT ROOSEVELT: "Don't be afraid, gentlemen; he will hurt only the crooks."

From the *Saturday Globe* (Utica, N. Y.)

THE USUAL VICTIM

From the *Herald* (New York)

Out of the intense discussion of that period, several plans of financial reform were evolved; and these had much debate during the ensuing Presidential campaign. Thus Mr.

VACATION TIME ON SAGAMORE HILL

From the *Tribune* (Minneapolis)

PRESIDENT ROOSEVELT: "Uncle Sam, it seems to me that this tool ought to be used."

From the *Tribune* (Minneapolis)

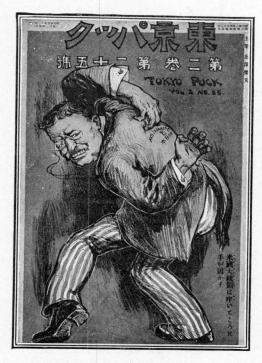

UNFORTUNATELY, PRESIDENT ROOSEVELT'S
ARMS ARE NOT LONG ENOUGH

From *Puck* (Tokio)

DISCUSSION IS BETTER THAN CONCUSSION

PRESIDENT ROOSEVELT: "Don't butt; let's talk it over."

From the *Eagle* (Brooklyn, New York)

Bryan made himself an advocate of the plan of guaranteeing bank deposits; and he secured the endorsement of this plan in the Democratic platform. Mr. Roosevelt and his administration agreed with most of the bankers that the guaranteeing of deposits would not be wise. They advocated, on their part, the establishment of a general system of postal savings-banks, so that if

THAT INTERVIEW AS IT WASN'T

ADMIRAL YAMAMOTO: "Good morning, Mr. President. We are going to have a war——"

PRESIDENT ROOSEVELT: "What's that?"

ADMIRAL YAMAMOTO: "We are going to have a warm day to-day."

PRESIDENT ROOSEVELT: "Oh, yes, yes! I think we are."

From the *Tribune* (Minneapolis)

PRESIDENT ROOSEVELT FINDS THE DENIZENS OF THE CANEBRAKE PREPARED
From the *Herald* (New York)

the people were afraid to deposit their savings in ordinary banks they could commit them to the care of the government under reasonable conditions. It was believed that this might be an especially effective thing in times of business panic or distrust.

In the last two years of the administration, the place of Postmaster-General was

RECIPROCITY
(One good lift deserves another.)
From the *Journal* (Minneapolis)

"WHEREAT I WAS MUCH CAST DOWN."—Theodore Roosevelt, "Hunting Big Game"
From the *Herald* (New York)

" Now, Mr. Railroadman, stock watering must stop—   Rates are too high—

They must come down—   Safety must be guaranteed—

I hope I impress my meaning on you—   Good day !"

RAILROAD LEGISLATION
From *Collier's Weekly*

THE VERY SIMPLE MESSAGE OF THE BIG
STICK. HE WHO RUNS MAY READ
From the *Tribune* (Minneapolis)

AN IMPREGNABLE SHIELD
From the *Gazette-Times* (Pittsburg)

filled by Mr. George von L. Meyer, who had served as ambassador at more than one leading European capital. Mr. Meyer bent all his energies toward securing the adoption by Congress of the postal savings-bank scheme; and although its success was deferred, there was every assurance that postal savings-banks would be established in the very near future. The plan was endorsed by the Republican national convention, and Congress accordingly passed the bill, with Mr. Taft and the Postmaster-General (Frank Hitchcock) also favoring it, early in 1910.

Mr. Roosevelt had managed through these years of high pressure and varied activity to avoid those effects of strain and over-work that few men have been able to escape whose responsibilities are great and whose duties are incessant. His, through the Presidential years, was always the clear, strong mind of the man who sleeps well, takes his exercise, and wards off the disease called worry.

Thus, as the panic came on Mr. Roosevelt was on his way back to Washington from a bear hunt in the Louisiana canebrakes. These absences were always well-planned, never interfered with public business, associated themselves with helpful visits to different parts of the country, and kept the President physically able to meet the tasks that only a strong man could survive.

That period of Mr. Roosevelt's Presidency was one in which his dominant note of justice and public duty was of more value to the country than any other tone or quality could have been. Whether the civil service, the national forests, tariff reciprocity with European countries, naval growth, insular questions, canal problems at Panama, an army and race theme like the Brownsville affair, or any other of a hundred topics was under consideration, Mr. Roosevelt brought to bear in every case the power of a vigorous mind and conscience. He saw in a clear, broad manner the thing that was right to be done, and demanded of Congress and the country the ethical solution and no other.

CHAPTER XXII

Refusing a Third Term

NOTHING like the Roosevelt third-term movement had ever before been known in American history. The struggle to give President Grant a third term was entered upon by his friends and political beneficiaries, in the very face of a disapproving national and party sentiment. But the movement to give Roosevelt a third term

PRESIDENTIAL TRANSPORTATION.—Both cartoons on this page are from the *Journal*, Minneapolis

THE G. O. P. ELEPHANT: "Come, Mr. President, I'll furnish you another free ride if you'll just get aboard."

THE HOUSE-HUNTERS (BRYAN, TAFT, AND FAIRBANKS)

BRYAN: "That house looks good to me, if the present occupant really expects to give it up."

JUST A LITTLE BIT NERVOUS

THE ELEPHANT: "I don't like the looks of that fellow, Theodore. You'd better stay with me till I get past 1908."—From the *Saturday Globe* (Utica)

was national and almost irresistible, and its successful resistence was due to his own firm will and the use of his prestige and power to secure a different result.

Naturally the Republican party desired success, and it was sure to win under his leadership. But he had made his announcement on election night in 1904, and he saw no good reason for changing his mind. He was, of course, plainly bound not to seek in any way a renomination, or to abet the movement. There was, however, no reason of honor or good faith that could have prevented his taking the oath of office and serving again, if he had been nominated and elected.

ALTHOUGH PRESIDENT ROOSEVELT HAS "IRREVOCABLY" REFUSED THE THIRD TERM NOMINATION, IT MAY COME TO THIS IN 1908.

From the *Spokesman-Review* (Spokane)

THE HUNTER HUNTED
From the *Journal* (Minneapolis)

"MARTIN LUTHER" ROOSEVELT

From *Puck.* Copyright, 1907. By permission

CÆSAR'S NO!

From *Puck*. Copyright 1908. By permission.

The President of the United States exercises in reality a greater power than do the hereditary rulers of monarchical countries. A masterful and positive President like Mr. Roosevelt, though loyal in all intent to the Constitution, drives swiftly to the ends he deems wise and right, and builds up for the executive an authority and an influence that tend to permeate the whole government. So popular a President as Roosevelt influences political situations in the States, and without any such precise purpose may bring under his moral sway many men in the Congresses he has helped to elect. He fills vacancies in the federal judiciary,—from the Supreme Bench to the district judgeships in all the States; and without a thought of undue influence over the judiciary, he may name a good many judges of his own way of thinking.

Thus the power of a strong President is cumulative; and there is wisdom and safety in the tradition that limits the President to a consecutive period of eight years. Mr. Roosevelt had not read American history amiss. If we had been in the thick of a great foreign war, and the country regardless of party had insisted upon his taking another term, he might have seen a sufficient reason for remaining at his post. But the country had an abundance of trained and capable men, and there was some reason to think that

TEDDY AND HIS PRESIDENTIAL SLATE
From the *American* (Nashville)

RELIEVING THEIR ANXIETY
(The aspirants for the Presidential nomination pressing Mr. Roosevelt to repeat his declaration that he would not run again.)
From the *Evening Star* (Washington)

the time had come for a President of a different temperament. Few people will ever understand how great a pressure Mr. Roosevelt resisted. Even those politicians who were thought to be opposing him were constantly pressing the idea upon his attention. After it had become certain that Taft would win as against any of the other candidates, there was a renewed effort to nominate Roosevelt, both to make the election easier and also to clear the field for 1912.

THE COUNTRY IS BACK OF HIM
Go ahead, Teddy; whichever path you choose you have U. S. back of you.
From the *Journal* (Minneapolis)

From the *Eagle* (Brooklyn, N. Y.)

THE PRESIDENT AND THE GOVERNORS—ALSO MR. BRYAN

(Mr. Roosevelt had called the Governors of the States and others into a great conference at the White House in May, 1908, to consider the preservation of natural resources.)

From the *Herald* (Washington)

A NATURAL RESOURCE

(Speaking of conserving our natural resources, Governor, do YOU think he could be induced to accept a third term?)

From the *Press* (New York)

FIRST OF ALL

From the *Eagle* (Brooklyn, N. Y.)

YOU'VE GOT TO REFORM YOUR EXTRAVAGANT
HABITS, OLD MAN
From the *Herald* (New York)

THE GOVERNORS!
(Were there moving pictures for the Governors?)
From the *Eagle* (Brooklyn, N. Y.)

PRESERVE THE FORESTS
From the *Eagle* (Brooklyn, N. Y.)

CHAPTER XXIII

Helping to Choose His Successor

MR. TAFT'S candidacy was not of his own seeking, neither was it arbitrarily forced upon the party by Mr. Roosevelt. It was the result of much consultation; and Mr. Taft, who would have preferred to return to the federal bench, became a candidate only because it was the prevailing view of the administration and the party that he was the most available man. Until the very last moment, there were great numbers of Republicans who clung to the hope that the convention would be stampeded for Mr. Roosevelt.

NOT A WEAKLING
From the *Evening World* (New York)

"HE'S ALL RIGHT"
From the *Evening Mail* (New York)

There were those who said that while Roosevelt himself would be acceptable to them, they did not approve of his dictating the choice of his successor. Governor Hughes had entered upon a brilliant record in New York, and it was decided by a majority of the New York delegation that his name should be presented at the Chicago convention as a candidate for Presidential honors. Senator Knox was the favorite son of Pennsylvania, and his name also was offered to the convention. Vice-President Fairbanks had the endorsement of his own State of Indiana, and some strength in other parts of the country.

Speaker Cannon had the great State of Illinois behind him, although he himself regarded his Presidential boom in the light of a mere personal compliment, and was ready to support Taft. The delegation from Wisconsin was instructed to present the name of Senator La Follette by way of reminding the convention of the turn in that gentleman's fortunes since the refusal of the convention of 1904 to seat him and his friends.

THE COURTSHIP OF BILL TAFT

PRISCILLA (the Republican party) : "Why don't you speak for yourself, Theodore?"

From *Puck.* Copyright, 1907. By permission

THE SHADOW ON THE WHITE HOUSE GROUNDS
From *Judge* (New York)

But Mr. Roosevelt fully realized that if the convention were deadlocked by reason of the conflicting claims of too many favorite sons, the outcome would inevitably be his own re-nomination. He bent all his energies, therefore, toward the securing of enough pledged

SECRETARY TAFT (to the President): "What's that blamed racket ahead, Theodore?"
(Secretary Taft does not find the trip to the White House devoid of adventure and opposition)
From the *Saturday Globe* (Utica)

LOADING THE BAND WAGON
From the *Spokesman-Review* (Spokane)

PRETTY GOOD AT "WINNING THE WEST"
HIMSELF
From the *Blade* (Toledo)

A LIVELY CONVENTION
(The President interested in the New York State
Convention.)
From the *World* (New York)

"THE THIN RED LINE OF HEROES" IN THE CONVENTION OF 1908
(The Taft delegates standing firm in the face of the tremendous enthusiasm for Roosevelt.)

From *Collier's Weekly*

THE "BIG STICK" WAS THERE
From the *Eagle* (Brooklyn, New York)

DEE-LIGHTED; OR, THE RINGMASTER
From the *Eagle* (Brooklyn, New York)

TAFT'S WRITING MASTER
From the *World* (New York)

**MR. ROOSEVELT GETS THE CHICAGO NEWS
WITH EVIDENT DELIGHT**
From the Philadelphia *Inquirer*, June 10

delegates to nominate Mr. Taft; and so the thing was accomplished. It was regarded by the country as an endorsement of the Roosevelt administration, and a determination to continue the Roosevelt policies.

For Mr. Taft had been a very conspicuous and highly trusted member of the administration, and at all times one of Mr. Roosevelt's two or three closest advisers. Mr. Roosevelt had a very high opinion of all his cabinet officers, but for the statesmanship of

THE GREATEST LEADER OF THEM ALL
From the *Herald* (New York)

THE PRESIDENT (to Bryan) : " You'll call me papa, will you? "
From the *Journal* (Detroit)

Mr. Root and Mr. Taft he had an especial regard. He ranked them with the great men of the early period of the Republic in respect of attainments, experience and constructive statesmanship.

" WE'VE BOTH HAD A PERFECTLY CORKING GOOD TIME ! "
From the *Eagle* (Brooklyn, N. Y.)

" HE BEGAN IT, TEACHER "—(Messrs. Hearst, Roosevelt, Bryan, and Kern in the campaign)
(The National Schoolmaster is somewhat indignant at the prevalence of mudslinging.)
From the *Saturday Globe* (Utica)

ROPED!

From the *Spokesman-Review* (Spokane)

Governor Hughes, who might have had the Vice-Presidency, was unwilling to accept it, and the New York delegation secured the convention's approval of the Hon. James S. Sherman. The ticket of Taft and Sherman was regarded as a little more conservative than Roosevelt himself, and the Democrats were ready to try their chances again under Mr. Bryan's leadership.

The old opposition to Bryan within the Democratic party had largely disappeared. There was a strong feeling that the ticket of Bryan and Kern might win against that of Taft and Sherman. Mr. Roosevelt as President could not, of course, go on the stump, but he took an intense and active interest in the work of the campaign, and did his best to refute the claims of Mr. Bryan that he, rather than Taft, was the true exponent of Roosevelt's progressive policies. The election of Mr. Taft was universally hailed as another Roosevelt victory.

It was a notable thing that both Taft and Bryan were presented to the country by their chief exponents as true and fit successors of Roosevelt, in respect of their doctrines and policies and of their personal attitude toward their fellow-citizens at large. The whole campaign as conducted on both sides,—even though it developed the usual asperities and heated accusations,—was in reality a tribute to the character of Roosevelt as a national figure who summed up the general aim and common belief of all honest and right-minded men, regardless of party.

The controversies of the campaign were not about fundamental things. The Republicans were accused of receiving campaign contributions from Wall Street,—with considerable truth, no doubt,—and the opponents of Mr. Taft were annoyed by disclosures connecting some of them with a certain Trust then under government prosecution. But

THE PRESIDENTIAL HANDICAP!—From the *Constitution* (Atlanta)

(Mr. Bryan is in doubt whether he is running against Mr. Taft or Mr. Roosevelt.)

these things were mere incidents, inevitable always in national campaigns. The Roosevelt administration was again before the country for endorsement. Taft was part and parcel of that administration, was the choice of Mr. Roosevelt, and was fully ratified by the party. And the country in the election once more gave a vote of its confidence in government of the Rooseveltian stamp.

ALONE I DIDN'T DO IT

MR. TAFT (breathless but triumphant): "Thank you, Teddy!"—From *Punch* (London)

ROOSEVELT'S BIGGEST BUBBLE

From *Pasquino* (Turin)

THE DISPUTED TITLE—WHO OWNS IT?

(A cartoon expressing the idea that the great issue of Roosevelt's administration had to do with the attempt of privileged and corporate wealth to control the country's resources and policies.)

CHAPTER XXIV

Last Phases of the Administration

M R. ROOSEVELT had by no means secured ready acquiescence by Congress in all of his policies, and his last year was full of storm and controversy. Thus in the session before the election of Mr. Taft he had laid down a program of rapid battleship construction, less than half of which had been endorsed. Nevertheless he had seen our navy grow to formidable dimensions.

Early in 1908, he had sent a great battleship fleet, under Admiral Evans, to make a tour of both South American coasts, then to cross the Pacific to Honolulu, Japan, the Philippines, and China, and to return by way of Australia, the Suez Canal, and the Mediterranean. This project was bitterly criticised, but it was most fortunate in its outcome.

Anti-Japanese riots in California had stirred up some feeling of antagonism to the United States among the more ignorant masses in Japan. It was predicted that if our ships entered Asiatic waters, they would encounter those of Japan in hostile action. As it turned out, the fleet was received with enthusiasm wherever it went, and nowhere more than in Japanese waters. Its visits of courtesy at the South American ports, and in the Far East, were felicitous in their strengthening of friendly ties with all the countries whose seaports were entered upon the route.

For a full year before the end of his term Mr. Roosevelt was using leisure moments

CONGRESS REFUSES TO APPROPRIATE WHAT THE PRESIDENT RECOMMENDS FOR NEW SHIPS, AND THE CARTOONIST ATTRIBUTES A SMILE TO JAPAN

From the *Evening Telegram* (New York)

T. "VESUVIUS" ROOSEVELT

(Referring to Mr. Roosevelt's tremendous activity.)

From *Collier's Weekly*

ROOSEVELT TO VISIT AFRICA

(And the Jungle Folk won't ratify.)

From the *Press* (Philadelphia)

to plan his trip to Africa and to make thorough preparations for his expedition. His eager looking forward to a year of adventures in a new field strengthened his courage for the public business that was pressing upon his attention. The prosecution of the Central and Southern Pacific railroads had been entered upon with a view to breaking up the combination they had formed.

A great action was pending for the dissolution of the Standard Oil Company as an illegal trust. Meanwhile one of Mr. Roosevelt's judicial appointees, Judge Landis, had imposed an enormous fine upon the Standard Oil Company for violation of the law against rebates; and Judge Grosscup, of the Circuit Court, had reversed Judge Landis' decision. During the campaign the relations of the Standard Oil Company to the press and to politics were a topic of violent controversy. The decision of Judge Landis was regarded by the business world as too drastic altogether, and there had grown up a feeling that Mr. Roosevelt was pressing with undue relentlessness a crusade against large business interests.

Whether or not there was good reason for this feeling, it involved the last year of Mr. Roosevelt's incumbency in heated argument and more show of temper and feeling than had been aroused at any previous stage in his career. At one time it had been thought that Mr. Roosevelt, in declining a third term

SIMPLIFIED SPELLING

(Apropos of the New York Senatorial situation and the report that Mr. Root may succeed Senator Platt in 1909, and that Mr. Roosevelt may succeed Senator Depew in 1911.)

From the *Herald* (Rochester)

A LITTLE LEGAL ARGUMENT WITH GROSSCUP

(Referring to the Standard Oil case)

From *Judge*

as President, might accept a seat in the United States Senate. The term of Senator Platt was to expire on March 4, at the same time as that of the President. But Mr. Roosevelt, although at one time this idea appealed to him, had definitely rejected it, and Secretary Root was the unopposed choice of his party in New York for the Senatorial toga.

The last annual message sent to Congress by Mr. Roosevelt in December, 1908, was a document of great length, devoted in the main to a recapitulation of the views and policies which had so strongly characterized his administration. His State papers had been much more extensive, and his formal utterances to Congress and the public more frequent, than those of any of his predecessors in the Executive office. The message did not serve to abate controversy or to soothe the worn and inflamed nerves of railway presidents or Wall Street bankers. Business was in the dumps, and some one must be blamed.

THE STATIONARY CRUSADER

PRESIDENT ROOSEVELT: "FOLLOW ME!" (or 35,000 words to that effect). See the President's message to Congress.

From *Punch* (London)

Congress in the previous session had undertaken to limit the President in the use of secret service funds placed at his disposal for the detection of crime; and the scathing comment made by the President in his message was ill-received in both legislative chambers. Attempts were made to expunge sections of the message before receiving it and entering it upon the record of Congress. However absurd such proposals might have been, they pointed to a certain bitterness and strain that was to affect the relations of the

THE UNITED STATES OF CENTRAL AMERICA,—A GERMAN VIEW

PRESIDENT ROOSEVELT: "Yes, yes, in union there is strength."

From *Kladderadatsch* (Berlin)

HANDS ACROSS THE SEA! AS CONGRESS SEES IT!

From the *Constitution* (Atlanta)

"WILL YOU PLEASE HUSH?"
From the *Herald* (New York)

Chief Magistrate and the law-making body through the remaining three months of Mr. Roosevelt's term.   The attempt of Congress to punish Roosevelt for his message was not successful and produced in the public mind a reaction in his favor.

ROUGH ON CATS
(The House and the Senate, before and after the
Presidential message current is turned on.)
From *Puck.*   Copyright 1908.   By permission

THE WATER'S FULL OF 'EM
From the *Globe* (New York)

"ONE WORD MORE."—AN ENGLISH VIEW

PRESIDENT ROOSEVELT (to Central African fauna) :
"Half a moment, while I just throw this off, and
then I'm with you."

From *Punch* (London)

One of the controversies of that session
had to do with the President's old subject,
the civil service. In passing a law providing for the taking of the Census of 1910,
Congress had disregarded the President's
advice that the thousands of extra census

ROOSEVELT'S FAREWELL MESSAGE POINTS
THE WAY

(President Roosevelt, in his last annual message
to Congress, makes many recommendations pointing
toward the betterment of social and industrial conditions in the United States.)

From the *Evening Herald* (Duluth)

employees should be appointed under civil
service rules. In this controversy Mr.
Roosevelt finally triumphed.

WHO WILL BELL THE CAT?
From the *North American* (Philadelphia)

"AFTER YOU!"

SENATE AND HOUSE (tremulously) : "You go first,
my dear sir."

(Congress took offense at some passages in the
President's annual message, and resolved to "re-
buke" him.)

From the *Eagle* (Brooklyn, N. Y.)

IT WILL
END THIS
SIDE UP.

TILLMAN

HOUSE

SENATE

(This idea of the result of the controversy between the President and Congress seems to prevail in the minds of a great many people.)

From the *Ohio State Journal* (Columbus)

He had also succeeded in extending the principle of the merit system to the retention of postmasters appointed to the smaller or fourth-class offices. During all his seven and a half years in the Presidency he had been able, in one way after another, to extend the

SPANKED!

(The spanking has evidently hurt "Pa Congress" more than it has the husky lad.)

From the *North American* (Philadelphia)

CONGRESS ASSUMES A FIRM ATTITUDE

From the *Daily News* (Chicago)

NOT SO EASY!

(Trying to hit the head,—a new Congressional game.)

From the *Inquirer* (Philadelphia)

sphere and improve the working of the civil-service rules, and thus to reduce the evils of the spoils system to comparatively few and small areas.

Several months before his retirement from office it had been announced that his literary activities would be resumed, and that his African experiences would be productive of a series of articles to be published in *Scribner's Magazine*. It was further made known that he would have a regular connection, as a frequent writer and contributing editor,

PROTECTING THE CIVIL SERVICE

From the *Pioneer Press* (St. Paul)

UNCLE SAM (on the side bench): "If there's anything I like, it's an old-fashioned game of 'shinny'!"

From the *Pioneer Press* (St. Paul)

TROUBLES BEGIN

(There will be the dickens to pay in the Fourth Estate before long.)—From the *Sun* (Baltimore)

with the *Outlook*, of New York, a widely read weekly periodical edited by Dr. Lyman Abbott. These announcements are reflected in two or three of the cartoons reproduced in the present chapter of our narration.

What may be regarded as the final controversy of his administration had to do with certain newspaper attacks upon the honesty of men connected with the purchase of the French Panama company's assets and the beginnings of our work on the canal.

Mr. Roosevelt had made great progress with the work at Panama. He had abandoned the original plan of constructing the canal under the direction of a board of engineers chosen from civil life and railroad

WHEN TEDDY BECOMES AN EDITOR
From the *Times-Star* (Cincinnati)

" ISN'T IT A DAISY?"

(Apropos of the review of the American battleship fleet by President Roosevelt on its return from the round-the-world trip, February 22, 1909.)
From the *Record* (Philadelphia)

WHY GO TO AFRICA FOR BIG GAME?

From the *Plain Dealer* (Cleveland)

work, and had turned it over to engineer officers of the regular army, with the most fortunate results. He looked upon the Panama enterprise as in some respects the crowning work of his administration; and he could not allow libels upon the honesty and good faith of the government and its agents, as respects the Panama Canal, to pass unnoticed.

The charges had involved, by express mention, well-known men closely related to the President and to the President-elect; and the charges had thus reflected upon the honor both of Mr. Roosevelt and of Mr. Taft, who, as Secretary of War, was in immediate charge of Panama affairs. Libel suits were entered by direction of President Roosevelt, and while

STEADY, TEDDY!
(This also refers to attacks mentioned above.)
From the *Eagle* (Brooklyn, N. Y.)

CHRISTMAS CARDS—From the *Eagle* (Brooklyn, N.Y.)
(President Roosevelt's compliments to certain newspapers which printed the Panama Canal charges.)

ROOSEVELT WARNS THE CANOEIST (CALIFORNIA) THAT RAPIDS AND ROCKS ARE AHEAD
From the *Leader* (Cleveland)

their prosecution was eventually abandoned, they were successful in their essential purpose. The prompt action taken by Mr. Roosevelt had secured complete retractions; and no stain had been left upon a page of our history that must always be memorable, and should, therefore, be without spot or tarnish.

PRESIDENT ROOSEVELT AND THE PRESIDENT-ELECT ENTERING THEIR CARRIAGE AT
THE WHITE HOUSE IN A SNOWSTORM ON MARCH 4, TO GO TO THE CAPITOL

CHAPTER XXV

Stepping Out of the White House

From *Puck*. Copyrighted 1908. By Permission

I'VE HAD A PERFECTLY CORKING TIME!

I F any man had ever seen Mr. Roosevelt in a mood of dejection or disheartenment, the fact had never been revealed. He was always the man of confidence and strong heart. It was not that he took his responsibilities recklessly, but he never allowed them to burden or weigh him down. There was never a day, however difficult, when he was not prepared to say of the Presidency, "I like my job," or to declare to friends and foes alike, "I am having a perfectly corking time."

IN THE WHITE HOUSE ATTIC, AS MOVING TIME APPROACHES

Mr. Roosevelt: "I wonder how much of this stuff Bill wants me to leave behind?"

From the *Saturday Globe* (Utica)

Doubtless this was due in large part to his great physical vitality, to the evenness and regularity of his habits of life and work, and to the firmness of a nervous system that was not, like those of most other men, subject to reaction after excitement. In the language of a White House usher, who had served through several administrations, "there

LETTERS FROM THE PEOPLE

From the *Daily Tribune* (Chicago)

was never any man like him for hard work; yet no matter how late he was at it every night, he came downstairs each morning as fresh as the dew upon the roses." If Mr. Roosevelt ever had any days or hours of illness, the secret never leaked out.

All his work was planned well in advance and finished easily on time. If he had a speech-making tour ahead of him, his dates were well arranged, and the speech to be made at each place had been carefully drafted and put on paper. Some Presidents had never found time while in office to read a book. Mr. Roosevelt always kept up with current literature, and was always digging into more or less recondite fields of history and science. He read whole libraries while in the White House, although no one knows how he found the time. He was conversant with early Celtic literature and with the sagas of the Teutonic North. He was more

THE NEWSPAPER MEN AND CARTOONISTS LA-MENTING MR. ROOSEVELT'S LEAVING THE WHITE HOUSE.
From the *News-Tribune* (Duluth)

thoroughly familiar than any other American with all books relating in a general way to sportsmanship, travel, and natural history. His constant devotion to the interests and concerns of his family had kept him acquainted also with the books that interest young people and children.

At the moment of his leaving the White House and starting on his adventurous journey to Africa he was, without doubt, more completely and freshly informed about Afri-

PASSING ON THE TORCH

("Let at least the satisfaction be ours that we have carried onward the lighted torch in our own day and generation. If we do this, then, as our eyes close, and we go into the darkness, and other hands grasp the torch, at least we can say that our part has been borne well and valiantly."—From Roosevelt's Lecture at Oxford.)

From the *Herald* (Syracuse)

PRESIDENT ROOSEVELT, AT THE LINCOLN FARM IN KENTUCKY, FEBRUARY 12, 1909

ROOSEVELT AT A LINCOLN DINNER IN NEW YORK
From the *Evening Mail* (New York)

can hunting,—in so far as knowledge could come from the reading of books and conversation with sportsmen and travelers,—than any other man in the world. He left the White House with no regrets, and with a sense of having served the country to the best of his ability. And somehow the world did not think of him as a man passing into retirement, or as one who had run his race and finished his course. Everybody was asking what Roosevelt would do next.

On February 12, less than a month before Mr. Roosevelt retired from the Presidency, he went to Hodgenville, Kentucky, to speak

WELL BEGUN AND WELL DONE
From the *Evening Mail* (New York)

at the farm where Abraham Lincoln was born, a hundred years before. His tribute to Lincoln on that occasion was, in rhetorical form, the most perfect speech he had ever prepared. Its portrayal of Lincoln's devotion to duty and high qualities as a great President was in some sense a revelation of Mr. Roosevelt's own ideals. It seemed to reflect something of the spirit in which, from his entrance into the political life of New York in 1882, through all his successive experiences, to the end of his term in the White House, he had given his own best courage and best effort for what he believed to be right causes.

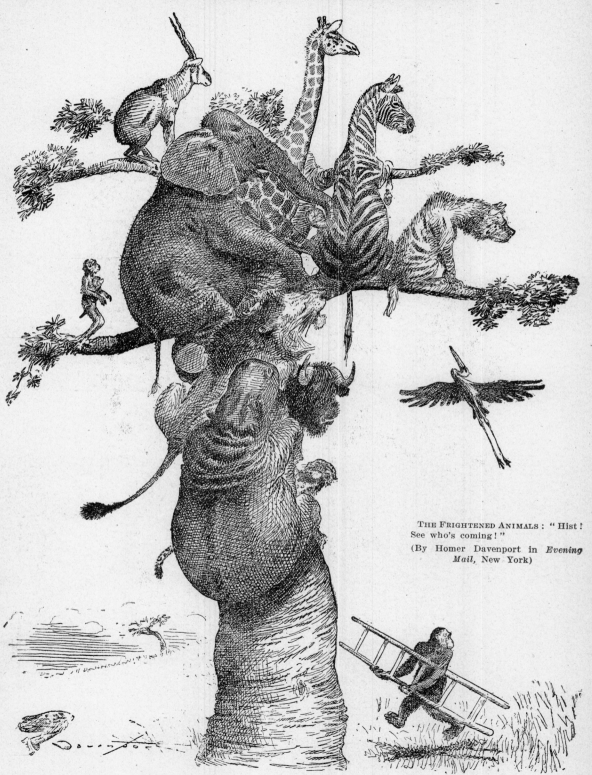

THE FRIGHTENED ANIMALS: "Hist! See who's coming!"

(By Homer Davenport in *Evening Mail*, New York)

CHAPTER XXVI
The Faunal Naturalist in Africa

EVEN in Africa Mr. Roosevelt was in a certain sense an official of the United States Government. He was the head of a scientific expedition, authorized by the Smithsonian Institution, to obtain faunal specimens for the National Museum. His expenses were otherwise provided for, but his mission was public and official. His preliminary report, made to Dr. Walcott as head of the Smithsonian, was forwarded from Khartum when the expedition disbanded.

MEETING OF SOVEREIGNS IN THE CENTER OF AFRICA

HIS MAJESTY, THE KING OF THE DESERT: "In the name of that Nobel whose prize covers you with glory, O Teddy, I implore you to spare other thousands of my subjects."

From *Pasquino* (Turin)

THEODORUS AFRICANUS

From the *World* (New York)

TEDDY AT HOME IN AFRICA

(This is a specimen of a great number of drawings by American cartoonists in the summer and fall of 1909, humorously associating Mr. Roosevelt with the fauna of Africa.)

From the *Press* (Pittsburg)

ROOSEVELT: "Oh, this is bully! Just think of poor Taft back home wrestling with Congress."

From the *News-Tribune* (Duluth)

BWANA TUMBO

("Bwana Tumbo," the name given to Mr. Roosevelt by the African natives, means "Big Chief," and the cartoonist here gives us his idea of Mr. Roosevelt arrayed in that character.)

From the *World* (New York)

Mr. Roosevelt has fortunately given us, first in magazine articles in *Scribner's* and then in permanent form as a notable volume, under the title "African Game Trails," an account of his experiences and achievements from the time of his leaving New York, March 23, 1909, to his arrival at Cairo in March, 1910. No quest of wild creatures was ever more carefully planned or better justified by its purposes, its methods, and its results. Its success was beyond Mr. Roosevelt's ardent expectations.

MR. ROOSEVELT'S REAL HEROISM

From the *Inter-Ocean* (Chicago)

The first of two results that will best serve to give this expedition a place of its own, memorable and influential, must be the vast collection of African animals and birds that will be the chief treasure of the National Museum at Washington and that will be familiar to young Americans for generations to come. The second result must be the book itself,—written by Mr. Roosevelt while on the ground,—constituting one of the best volumes in the long series of his writings, and also one of the most valuable contributions to the literature of animal life and natural conditions in Africa.

Most of Mr. Roosevelt's experiences were in British East Africa and Uganda, where he came in contact also with British officials, missionaries, and ranchmen, whose fondness for the African wilderness recalled to him his own experiences as a ranchman on the borders of Dakota and Montana. He was

THE AGE OF ACHIEVEMENT
From the *World* (New York)

MISSING THE FUN
From the *Eagle* (Brooklyn, N. Y.)

(The announcement of Dr. Cook's discovery of the Pole was brought to Roosevelt in Africa, and he received the news with mental reservation and in silence. A few days later the Peary announcement came, and he instantly cabled his enthusiastic congratulations. Commander Peary made his polar expedition in a ship named the *Roosevelt*.)

intensely interested in race questions, and in all phases of life and nature in the portions of Africa where he sojourned, hunted, and camped.

All of his experiences are set down in vivid form upon the fascinating pages of his book, just as other volumes of his tell us with swift and firm narration — but with the discursiveness of a naturalist who sees the whole environment — all about the hunting of game in our own Western wilds. The habit, to which we have already made reference, of giving immediate, vivid, and

REMINISCENT.—From the *Herald* (Washington)

HUNTING A CANDIDATE

(Previous to the New York municipal campaign in 1909 there was some talk
of tendering the nomination for Mayor to Colonel Roosevelt.)

From *Coler's Bulletin* (Brooklyn, N. Y.)

charming literary form to all of his active experiences out of doors, is one of the very best things attributable to his early life in his frontier ranch-house, where he had good books and not too many of them, and the power to see a narrative worth telling in each well-considered expedition after bear, mountain lion, or other creatures of highland and plain.

Accompanying Mr. Roosevelt, as his fellow-members of the scientific Smithsonian African Expedition entrusted to his charge, were Messrs. Mearns, Heller, and Loring, American naturalists; and Messrs. Cunninghame and Tarlton, who were British experts on African hunting and travel. More than 11,000 specimens were secured for the National Museum, including nearly 5000 mammals,—most of them large, about 4000 birds, and a large number of reptiles and smaller creatures.

IN DANGER OF BEING KIDNAPPED

(Apropos of a statement by C. D. O'Brien, a prominent
St. Paul Democrat, that the Democratic party will nominate and elect Roosevelt President in 1912.)

From the *News-Tribune* (Duluth)

"BWANA TUMBO" FOR MAYOR

From the *Press* (New York)

UNANIMOUS
(Colonel Roosevelt laying a cornerstone at Kijabe, Africa.)
From the *Inter-Ocean* (Chicago)

IN AFRICA AND—IN THE UNITED STATES
From the *Journal* (Minneapolis)

The expedition would have been followed through Africa by an army of press representatives but for Mr. Roosevelt's stern insistence. So great, however, was the demand for news that there was some yielding to the tendency to manufacture it on the coast, or else to send to the European and American papers exaggerated tales based upon half-accurate rumors. There was no indis-

VALENTINE'S DAY IN AFRICA
From the *News* (Detroit)

THE FAUNAL NATURALIST AT WORK
From the *Traveler* (Boston)

MR. ROOSEVELT AND ONE OF HIS BIG LIONS

(From a photograph by Kermit Roosevelt in Theodore Roosevelt's "African Game Trails," published by Charles Scribner's Sons.)

criminate slaughter of animals, and no departure from the excellent plans originally made. Such plans, obviously enough, took into account all questions of climate, risk of illness, and sanitary precautions. Mr. Roosevelt was accompanied by his son, Mr. Kermit Roosevelt, whose skill and prowess as a hunter form a part of the true story of the expedition.

Mr. Roosevelt's habit of applying all proper means to the ends that he wished to secure was perfectly illustrated in the African expedition throughout. Every detail of the itinerary had been planned and every item of equipment had been considered to a nicety. Even the books that he meant to read were carefully selected in advance, and all bound in pigskin, forming a compact little library for entertainment, diversion, and intellectual stimulus in hours of leisure during the African twelvemonth.

Thus the results to which we have alluded,—namely, the great Smithsonian collection of African fauna and the admirable volume on "African Game Trails," together with the building up of physical vigor and the ripening of knowledge concerning colonial, imperial, and racial problems, as well as knowledge of natural history,—all these results, and many others, were not in the least matters of "Roosevelt luck" so-called, but were all of them matters of Roosevelt industry, perseverance, and faithful application of the right means to the desired ends.

The human family has grown very rapidly during the past century, in spite of that tendency to apply Malthusian checks which, —in highly civilized countries like France and the United States,—has led Mr. Roosevelt to utter warnings against what he has called "race suicide." And with the multiplication of the members of the human species there has naturally been growth in

THE END OF A REMARKABLE EXPEDITION
From *Hojas Selectas* (Barcelona)

the numbers of domesticated animals. But the wild creatures which had shared with man the vicissitudes of mundane existence have perforce become fewer in numbers and subject to conditions ever more precarious.

A knowledge of these fellow creatures,—their ways and struggles,—constitutes a very noble and interesting department of science. Mr. Roosevelt has taught the boys of America, and now also those of Europe as well, not merely to slaughter birds and beasts, but to know about them and to

MR. ROOSEVELT, RHINO AND BUSTARD
From a photograph by Kermit Roosevelt
In Theodore Roosevelt's "African Game Trails" published by Charles Scribner's Sons

MR. ROOSEVELT AS HE APPEARED IN EGYPT

have the true attitude of mind towards them. His relation towards these fellow creatures has always been humane, never cruel.

There is always struggle among the animals themselves, whether in the American wilderness or in the African jungle. And if mankind had not struggled against powerful beasts of prey, the human race must long ago have perished from the earth.

Mr. Roosevelt's teachings and example in all these things,—from the time of his college essays and studies as a naturalist, and his early Western hunting trips, down to his last great quest of animals in Africa,—have been of immeasurable value in leading young Americans to the love of enjoyment of out-of-door things, and away from pleasures and occupations that would enervate mind and body.

CHAPTER XXVII

Strenuously Visiting Old Europe

"TALK ABOUT BEING PRESIDENT!"

From the *Plain Dealer* (Cleveland)

THE expedition of our hunter and naturalist came to an end with its arrival and disbanding at Khartum, on March 14, 1910. Here his wife and daughter were awaiting Mr. Roosevelt, as were the representatives of many newspapers,

THE BIG STICK IN USE AGAIN

From the *Press* (Grand Rapids)

AS EGYPT SEES HIM

From the *Plain Dealer* (Cleveland)

THE AFRICAN COMET
(Due to hit New York June 18.)
From the *American* (New York)

BACK IN THE OLD PLACE
From the *Eagle* (Brooklyn, N. Y.)

both European and American. The remaining days of March were spent in Egypt; and April, May, and the early part of June were taken up with a memorable tour of Europe.

It is the object of this chapter chiefly to bring together some of the amusing caricatures and cartoons that were produced in consequence of a journey that caused more comment than any other of recent times. Our former chapters show how large a figure Mr. Roosevelt as President had become

A SITTER; OR, BIG GAME TO THE LAST

Mr. Roosevelt: "Steady, Kermit! We must have one of these."

From *Punch* (London)

THE SLEEPING CONSERVATIVE, DREAMING OF ROOSEVELT, SEES A "BACK FROM ELBA" NIGHTMARE!

From the *Plain Dealer* (Cleveland)

ROOSEVELT AS "CHANTECLER"
From the *World* (New York)

in the estimation of the world. It was not strange, therefore, that Europe should have manifested a keen interest in his visit, and that there should have been a general desire to extend a hearty welcome to the best-known and most typical

MR. PINCHOT'S CONFERENCE WITH COLONEL
ROOSEVELT IN EUROPE
From the *News* (Cleveland)

MAYBE MR. TAFT'S EARS DIDN'T TINGLE!
From the *Sun* (Baltimore)

KING HAAKON AND COLONEL ROOSEVELT IN ROYAL CARRIAGE LEAVING THE STATION
AT CHRISTIANIA

MR. AND MRS. ROOSEVELT AND THEIR DAUGHTER AT NAPLES

ROOSEVELT'S WORD TO EUROPE.—From *Pasquino* (Turin)

ROOSEVELT: "In the name of America I call upon you to disarm!"
EUROPEAN SOVEREIGNS (in chorus): "Why don't you begin yourself?"

of Americans as the opportunity offered.

In an address at the University of Egypt he told the Nationalists what preparation for self-government meant; and was naturally criti-

A STRENUOUS VISITATION OF OLD EUROPE
From the *Herald* (Boston)

CONQUERING CONTINENTS
From the *Times* (New York)

cised by hot-headed patriots for giving some excellent counsel. For the Egyptians to seek independence at the present time would mean chaos and ruin; and Mr. Roosevelt's words of praise for England's usefulness in Egypt were wisely spoken, and at the time and place where they could serve the best use.

LIKE TO SEE ANYBODY BEAT THAT FOR TEN MINUTES' WORK
(Apropos of some expressions by Colonel Watterson on the subject of Roosevelt.)
From the *Pioneer Press* (St. Paul)

ALL THINGS TO ALL MEN
From the *American* (New York)

THE BARNUM OF HIMSELF.—*Fischietto*

(Ex-President Roosevelt, on his return from Africa, has traveled through Europe to show off his menagerie of stuffed animals. Why not capture him at Hamburg? The professional trainers could make the bunglers pay dear by taking him on a tour through the United States to make the Yankees open their eyes in amazement.)

WILL THIS BE THE CROWNING TRIUMPH?

(The cartoonist of *Fischietto,* an illustrated weekly published in Turin, is of opinion that an appropriate and up-to-date way for Colonel Roosevelt to return to the United States would be by means of an aeroplane.)

Mr. Roosevelt was received with honor and cordiality by rulers and by people throughout Italy. His visits in Naples and Rome were notable, and he found ovations awaiting him at Milan, Genoa, and Venice. He was received with the highest honors at Vienna; and at Budapest and elsewhere in Hungary there was boundless enthusiasm among a people who remembered well the story of

" HERE'S THE LION-HUNTER "
—And the stone lions are fleeing for their lives!
From *Kakas Márton* (Budapest)

" HE WAS NOT BORN A RULER, BUT, BETTER STILL, HE IS A BORN RULER "
From *Bolond Islok* (Budapest)

WELCOME, MR. ROOSEVELT

What is Roosevelt's daughter, say?
  Lady, lady, lady!
What is Kermit, smooth and gay?
  Pretty, pretty, pretty!
Who's our darling of to-day?
  Teddy, Teddy, Teddy!
What are we for Roosevelt play?
  Ready, ready, ready!

From *Klods-Hans* (Copenhagen)

(The *Floh*, Vienna's best known cartoon weekly, in its
"Roosevelt edition" pictures Uncle Sam announcing that
our "most glorious Presidents" have been Washington,
Monroe, Lincoln, McKinley, and Roosevelt.)

PEACE AT ANY COST

(Apropos of Colonel Roosevelt's address on peace at
Copenhagen)

From the *American* (New York)

MR. ROOSEVELT'S ADMIRATION FOR VIENNA

(According to *Floh*, Mr. Roosevelt was so charmed with
Vienna that he has decided to forego future American
honors and accept the position of Mayor of the Austrian
capital.)

HOLLAND'S CORDIAL RECEPTION

ROOSEVELT: "All this seems very familiar to me."
THE DUTCH NATION: "It is the home of your ancestors. You are thrice welcome."

From *Der Amsterdammer* (Amsterdam)

THE FRENCHMAN GETS A STRENUOUS SHAKE

ROOSEVELT (shaking hands vigorously with M. Briand,
to the latter's discomfort): "In democracies, my dear
Briand, it is necessary to be energetic."

From *Le Rire* (Paris)

"EMPHASIZING THE OBVIOUS" IN PARIS

MR. ROOSEVELT (addressing the Sorbonne): "Educated
folk know more than ignoramuses; peace is less bloody
than war; rich men are not poor; race suicide is one of
the causes of decline in population," etc.

From *Le Rire* (Paris)

SO UNUSUAL!

"How is this, my dear Teddy, you are going without
borrowing three or four hundred millions? Is it possible
that you were not satisfied with your reception?"

From *Le Rire* (Paris)

THE SCHOOLMASTER ABROAD

EXAMINER ROOSEVELT: "Kindergarten class in science
of government is now dismissed."

From the *World* (Toronto)

WAR AND PEACE IN HIS HANDS,—A POLISH VIEW

From *Mucha* (Warsaw)

THE COMING GUEST

THE KAISER: "You boys will have to eat in the kitchen
to-day; I expect company."

From the *Herald* (Syracuse)

GETTING NERVOUS AS TEDDY APPROACHES

THE KAISER (to his Chief of Police) : "You're sure the fire alarms are all O. K.?"

From the *Journal* (Detroit)

Kossuth's reception in the United States. The sympathy of Hungary was to be expected.

The many European cartoons that are reproduced in this chapter indicate at once the amusement, liking, and aroused curiosity of the intelligent public all the way from Italy to

ALL READY TO RECEIVE ROOSEVELT

From the *American* (New York)

THE COMPLIMENT SUPREME

From the *Eagle* (Brooklyn)

UNTER DEN LINDEN
From the *Tribune*
(Chicago)

BIRDS OF A FEATHER,—TEDDY AND THE KAISER
From the *Inquirer* (Philadelphia)

ROOSEVELT IN BERLIN

ROOSEVELT: "You are aware, my dear William, that I have already had an opportunity of speaking my mind to the other nations. In the interest of our work for peace I would recommend to you this exclusive use for the spiked helmet, especially in Alsace!"

From *Nebelspalter* (Zurich)

SONS OF THE WAR GOD
MARS: "Bless you, my children."
From the *Spokesman-Review* (Spokane)

"SPEAKING THROUGH EUROPE"
From *Kladderadatsch* (Berlin)

EMPEROR WILLIAM AND COLONEL ROOSEVELT AT DOBERITZ ON MAY 11

(It was on this occasion that the Emperor, addressing Colonel Roosevelt, said : "My friend, it is my great delight to welcome you in the presence of my guards and my army. I want you to realize that you are the first private citizen to review German troops." Then turning to the assembled officers, he said : "Gentleman, it is a great honor for us to have among us the distinguished Colonel of the American Rough Riders.")

MR. ROOSEVELT WITH AMBASSADORS BACON AND JUSSERAND AND OTHER DISTINGUISHED MEN AT THE TOMB OF NAPOLEON

Ein lieber Besuch.

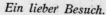

THE EX-PRESIDENT'S MODESTY

" Do not forget, gentlemen. that I am only a plain
American citizen."

From *Ulk* (Berlin)

ROOSEVELT AS THE " WILD HUNTER " IN THE
ROYAL GERMAN PALACE—From *Ulk* (Berlin)

Roosevelts Vortrag in Berlin:
„Die Pflichten des Bürgers einer konstitutionellen Monarchie"

„Mylords und Gentlemen! Erstens hat dieser Bürger das stolze
Selbstbewußtsein zu zeigen, das ihm sein auf die Volksvertretung
gestütztes persönliches Recht verleiht, dann aber auch jene Hingabe
zu beweisen, deren nur ein echt königstreues Gemüt fähig ist!

Mannhaft muß er selbst dem
Throne gegenüber mit Donner-
worten seine individuelle
Meinung vertreten —

andererseits muß ihn aber auch
jenes warme Gefühl für das
angestammte Herrscherhaus be-
seelen, das eine Folgeerscheinung
der Demut vor den gott-
gewollten Abhängigkeiten
darstellt.

Als Bürger eines konstitutio-
nellen Staates soll er hoch er-
haben über dem kleinlichen Ver-
langen nach höherer An-
erkennung stehn —

doch soll er trotzdem ein
Plätzchen auf seinem, zum
anderen Teil monarchisch
gesinnten Herzen freihalten,
wo ein Kranz beglückender
Ehrenzeichen und Dekorationen
jederzeit Raum findet! m. br.

ROOSEVELT'S BERLIN ADDRESS

(A German humorous view of Colonel Roosevelt making
his address at the University of Berlin, on May 12.)

From *Kladderadatsch* (Berlin)

THE COLONEL'S DASH THROUGH EUROPE

"Have you seen him passing by?"

From the *Eagle* (Brooklyn)

NOT WORRYING OVER THE VATICAN INCIDENT

ROOSEVELT: "I have been to Rome, and have not seen the Pope."

From *Der Floh* (Vienna)

(This, of course, is in no way expressive of Mr. Roosevelt's feeling, for he had hoped to pay his respects at the Vatican.)

TELLING HUNTER'S TALES IN THE WIGWAM ON THE SPREE

ROOSEVELT (to Chancellor Bethmann-Hollweg): "Picture my predicament, my dear Bethmann-Hollweg; on my right an alligator was preparing to rush at me; on my left crouched a lion; over me a vulture hovered, and under me crawled a rattlesnake,—how do you think I saved myself? By good luck I had with me a newspaper containing your election franchise proposal. I read it aloud, and the wild beasts promptly turned tail and fled in a panic. I was saved!"—From *Jugend* (Munich)

BACK TO EUROPE WITH HIS AFRICAN SPOIL

(The view of *Kladderadatsch*, Berlin)

Norway, and from Hungary to the British Isles. It was in Paris, on the 23d of April, that Mr. Roosevelt delivered his address on " Citizenship in a Republic," as had been planned long in advance. From Paris the journey was continued, by way of Belgium and Holland, to the Scandinavian countries. His reception in Holland was especially hearty because of his own Dutch ancestry. At Christiania, following visits and royal receptions in Copenhagen and Stockholm, he made an address

TEDDY'S LAST RESORT (Mr. Roosevelt had a temporary hoarseness in Germany)

(In order not to run the risk of again being without a voice through strain of speech-making, poor Roosevelt will have to rely for the moment upon the invention of another great American—illustrious Edison. For a premier such as he would like to be, this hoarseness is a great bore.)

From *Fischietto* (Turin)

LONGED-FOR LAURELS

The Kaiser: " Ah, Teddy, if I only could talk as you did before you got hoarse."

From *Kladderadatsch* (Berlin)

TEDDY IN EUROPE

" The critic of monarchs."

From *Kladderadatsch* (Berlin)

THE "FREEDOM" OF THE CITY

MR. ROOSEVELT: "Mornin', Brer Terrapin!"

CITY TURTLE: "Mornin', Colonel! Guess you ain't goin' to lie low and say nuffin?"

MR. ROOSEVELT: "Well, what do you think?"

From *Punch* (London)

Copyright by Brown Bros., N.Y

FROM A SNAPSHOT IN EUROPE

upon world peace, in recognition of his having received the Nobel Prize.

The death of King Edward of England changed his plans somewhat, but he proceeded to Berlin, where he was privately received and entertained by the Kaiser, in company with whom he reviewed a body of

NOT TAKING ANY CHANCES

(In advance of the great hunter's arrival in England, the public statuary has been surrounded by guards and duly labeled "Not to be Shot!")

From *Punch* (London)

German troops, and where on May 12 (the Emperor attending) he addressed the University of Berlin on "The World Movement."

In the meanwhile, President Taft had notified him by cable of his appointment as a special am-

THE CAMEL AND THE EYE OF A NEEDLE—From the *Daily Dispatch* (London)
TEDDY (to John Bull): "You'll never coax him with that soft stuff. Take a stick to him."

bassador to England to represent the United States at the funeral of King Edward. He arrived in London on May 16, and his ambassadorial rank, together with his own prestige, made him one of the most conspicuous of the personages who were in official attendance at the royal funeral. A few days later he received a degree at the University of Cambridge, and on May 31 he was granted the freedom of the city of London, making an address in the Guildhall, in which he discussed especially England's status in Egypt.

THE BISHOP BIRD: "Won't you come and have a shot at us?"
From the *Westminster Gazette* (London)

JOHN BULL AND HIS TEDDY BEAR
From the *Westminster Gazette* (London)

THE WISDOM OF THE WEST

From *Punch* (London)

"ENGLAND, AWAKE!"
From the *World* (New York)

THE ENTOMOLOGIST
From the *Sun* (Baltimore)

MOSES IN THE (JOHN) BULL RUSHES
(A new law-giver appears in the land of Egypt.)
From *Le Rire* (Paris)

MULTUM EX PARVO

FILIPINO (reading Mr. Roosevelt on the proper management of Egypt): "Splendid! There's nothing he don't know about empire! And to think that he picked it all up from me!"

("I advise you only in accordance with the principles on which I have myself acted in dealing with the Philippines."—Mr. Roosevelt at the Guildhall.)

From *Punch* (London)

JOHN BULL FROM MR. ROOSEVELT'S POINT OF
VIEW
From the *Morning Leader* (London)

JOHN BULL'S PARTING HANDSHAKE
From the *Inquirer* (Philadelphia)

BOTH HANDS FULL
(After the much-discussed Guildhall speech, for which
Colonel Roosevelt received both praise and blame.)
From the *Eagle* (Brooklyn)

His endorsement of a firm policy on the part of the British Government in the land of the Nile became a matter of world-wide comment and argument. The British Prime Minister, some time after Mr. Roosevelt's departure for America, commended the speech on the floor of Parliament; and it produced a visible effect upon public opinion as regards England's mission in Egypt and our own in the Philippines. On June 7, at the University of Oxford, he delivered the Romanes lecture, which was the primary occasion of his visit to England, his subject being "Biological Analogies in History." A day or two later he set sail for New York.

SAYING GOOD-BYE TO EUROPE
"For he's a jolly good fellow!"
From the *Post-Intelligencer* (Seattle)

EX-PRESIDENT ROOSEVELT AND MAYOR GAYNOR OF NEW YORK CITY

(As they appeared on the occasion of the Mayor's greeting to the returning traveler at the official reception,
June 18, 1910, at the Battery.)

CHAPTER XXVIII
His Home-Coming and Welcome

HOMEWARD BOUND
"This is my own, my native land"
From the *Times-Star* (Cincinnati)

land of opportunity and of promise, and Roosevelt's name had become familiar as that of the man typifying the best things in the life of the American people.

The European press had received Roosevelt with interest, curiosity, and expressions of amusement more or less polite. His address at the Guildhall, which was admirable in form and spirit, quite shocked the British newspapers because it was the conventional British thing to appear shocked. In reality, nobody was in the smallest degree perturbed or offended.

I N Europe the plain people had received Roosevelt gladly everywhere. The European enemies of America have always been among the rulers and privileged classes. The United States has meant to the workman and the peasant of Europe the

OLD EUROPE RESTING AT LAST!
From the *Inquirer* (Philadelphia)

"I CAN'T SEE HIM, BUT I THINK I CAN HEAR HIM!"
From the *Plain Dealer* (Cleveland)

UNCLE SAM'S TURN NEXT!

"MY COUNTRY, 'TIS OF THEE!"
From the *Sun* (Baltimore)

IN PASSING

(Colonel Roosevelt, on the homeward voyage, takes advantage of the opportunity to deliver a lecture to old Neptune on "How to Run the Ocean.")
From the *American* (New York)

SIGHTED!
From the *Evening World* (New York)

RELIEF IN SIGHT
From the *Herald* (Washington)

AWAITING THE TRAVELER'S RETURN
From the *Post* (Pittsburg)

NEW YORK TO MR. ROOSEVELT: "Good-morning, Colonel!"—From the *Eagle* (Brooklyn, N. Y.)

RELIEF!
From the *Daily News* (Chicago)

WONDER WHAT THEY ARE LOOKING FOR?
From the *Inquirer* (Philadelphia)

DELIGHTED!
From the *Journal* (Minneapolis)

BACK FROM ELBA
From the *News-Scimitar* (Memphis)

But much more important than Europe's casual impressions, and the comments of the European press, was the sort of effect upon the state of mind of his own countrymen that Mr. Roosevelt's return was destined to produce. His last year in the White House had been difficult, and many of the newspapers had been harsh in their criticisms. The President is a man of great power by virtue of the bearings his office has upon the fortunes of hundreds of thousands of men who are of some consequence in their own communities. When Mr. Roosevelt refused another term and his successor was duly elected people began to think of the man who was coming into power and who was already choosing his official associates, rather than of the man who was not only laying down the

THE UNITED STATES WILL PLEASE COME TO ORDER!
From the *Herald* (Washington)

INSURGENT AND REGULAR, BOTH: "You wait till Roosevelt gets here; he'll fix you!"
From the *Oregonian* (Portland)

UNCLE SAM'S "WELCOME HOME" TO ROOSEVELT

(Homer Davenport in New York *Evening Mail*)

From the *Eagle* (Brooklyn)

pressed themselves, with rather brutal frankness, as happy to have Mr. Roosevelt go to Africa. They were eager to enter upon the expected years of calmness and unruffled business prosperity that were sure to come with the wise and steady administration of Taft, succeeding the headstrong and turbulent years of the Rough Rider in leadership of the nation.

It is not the President alone, however, who makes our political and financial weather. Mr. Taft's first year was stormier than any one of Mr. Roosevelt's seven and a half years. This was for many reasons; some of which were subject to Mr. Taft's control. Many of them, however, were beyond his power.

It happened, nevertheless, that just as Wall Street and the people whose state of

sceptre of rule, but who was also going into a voluntary exile, banishing himself to the heart of Africa, in order that there might be no man able to say that Roosevelt out of office was still trying to order the affairs of the country.

There was widespread interest in his African movements, but only scanty news. Not one word of authorized interview, or of comment upon American affairs or his own intentions, did Mr. Roosevelt utter during his entire absence. Many business men throughout the country, led by Wall Street, had ex-

MUTUAL GREETING
From the *Times-Star* (Cincinnati)

"HURRAH FOR TEDDY!"
(The welcome awaiting him at the hands of the people.)
From *Collier's Weekly*

mind is determined by the business barometers had formed the habit of abusing Mr. Roosevelt with extreme exaggeration, even so had they in one short year begun to abuse Mr. Taft quite as unsparingly. And since Mr. Taft was the man at the helm, it was easy enough to forget the other man's faults and to wish that he were steering the ship again.

And so a good many of the men who had been willing to have Roosevelt exile himself, but who had not been willing in March, 1909, to go down the harbor to bid him God-

THE NON-PARTISAN RECEPTION
(In accordance with Colonel Roosevelt's wishes, his reception was entirely non-partisan.)
From the *Record* (Philadelphia)

HOME AGAIN!
From the *World* (New York)

HIS PROGRESS HOMEWARD

SWAMPING THE COLONEL!
From the *Press* (New York)

speed, were quite elated to find themselves appointed to serve on the large reception committee of June, 1910; and down the harbor they cheerfully went, to welcome Mr. Roosevelt back home with effusion, if not with life-long affection.

The country as a whole, however, welcomed him home with an enthusiasm and a devotion that were sincere beyond any doubt. He was greeted with an applause that rang true in every State and Territory. Nothing of its kind so impressive had ever been seen in New York as the crowds that lined the route of his drive from the Battery up Broadway to Central Park at high noon of June 18, 1910.

It would be easy to make up a volume of the clever and amusing cartoons drawn for the American newspapers in the few days just before and just after Mr. Roosevelt's

TAKING ON THE PILOT
From *Collier's Weekly*

From *Collier's Weekly*

arrival. We have selected a few of these, in
order to give some impression of the spirit
and character of the country's greeting. It
was deeply gratifying to Mr. Roosevelt to be
welcomed home with such heartiness; and
the little speech he made, in response to
Mayor Gaynor's formal but kindly words
of welcome, must be recorded in these pages
as belonging to our condensed chronicle of
Roosevelt's career. The speech in full was
as follows:

I thank you, Mayor Gaynor. Through you I thank
your committee, and through them I wish to thank
the American people for their greeting. I need
hardly say I am most deeply moved by the reception
given me. No man could receive such a greeting

Copyright, 1910, by Harper & Brothers

"MY BOY!"
(Uncle Sam's welcome to ex-President Roosevelt.)
From *Harper's Weekly*

Drawn by F. G. Cooper

THE RETURN FROM ELBA
From *Collier's Weekly*

UNCLE SAM: "How's the boy?"
From the *Inquirer* (Philadelphia)

FATHER KNICKERBOCKER: "Come to my arms, my beamish boy!"
From the *World* (New York)

without being made to feel both very proud and very humble.

I have been away a year and a quarter from America, and I have seen strange and interesting things alike in the heart of the frowning wilderness and in the capitals of the mightiest and most highly polished of civilized nations. I have thoroughly enjoyed myself, and now I am more glad than I can say to get home, to be back in my own country, back among the people I love.

And I am ready and eager to do my part, so far as I am able, in helping solve problems which must be solved if we of this the greatest democratic Republic upon which the sun has ever shone are to see its destinies rise to the high level of our hopes and its opportunities.

This is the duty of every citizen, but it is peculiarly my duty; for any man who has ever been honored by being made President of the United States is thereby forever after rendered the debtor of the American people, and is bound throughout his life to remember this as his prime obligation, and in private life as much as in public life, so to carry himself that the American people may never have cause to feel regret that once they placed him at their head.

On the following page is a picture of Mr. Roosevelt in the act of uttering these appropriate words. The meaning of the statement was clear beyond a doubt. Mr. Roosevelt meant as ex-President to serve his country as best he could, doing everything in his power to promote progress and justice, without seeking anything for himself.

UNCLE SAM: "Just as I expected, Teddy! Associating with Emperors and Kings hasn't changed you one particle!"—From the *Press* (New York)

EN ROUTE AGAIN
From the *World* (New York)

Photograph by the American Press Assn

MR. ROOSEVELT RESPONDING TO MAYOR GAYNOR'S ADDRESS

Photograph by Brown Bros.

THE WELCOMING CROWDS ON FIFTH AVENUE, NEW YORK, JUNE 18, 1910

WHEN TEDDY COMES MARCHING HOME
From the *Journal* (Detroit)

NEW YORK AT LAST!
From the *Jersey Journal* (Jersey City)

UNCLE SAM : " We were wondering what to do with you."
T. R. : " Leave that to me ! "—Philadelphia *Press*.

Photograph by Brown Bros.

THE ROUGH RIDERS GREETING THEIR COLONEL

HIS GREATEST HONOR

(Roosevelt's enthusiastic reception on landing at New York.)

From the *Herald* (Boston)

Photograph by the American Press Assn.

RECOGNIZING FRIENDS EN ROUTE

HOME AGAIN!
From the *Evening News* (Newark)

SAGAMORE HILL, MR. ROOSEVELT'S HOME, AS IT WAS IN THE SUMMER OF 1910

CHAPTER XXIX

An Ex-President in His Active Retirement

THE FAITH OF THE COMMON PEOPLE
"Now that Roosevelt is home again, every-
thing will be all right."
From the *North American* (Philadelphia)

GOODNESS! CAN THIS BE THE ORIGINAL BIG
STICK?
From the *Oregonian* (Portland)

FOR ex-Presidents there is no established code of duty or of eti-
quette. It has come to be well
understood that a Vice-President should
be dignified, without seeming to be as-
piring or expectant, and without allow-
ing himself to be influential. What ex-
Presidents, however, ought to do, besides remembering that they are to set
an example of dignity and of unselfish
devotion to country, is a question that
has always been debated but never
conclusively answered.

There are those who would make our
ex-Presidents Senators for life. There

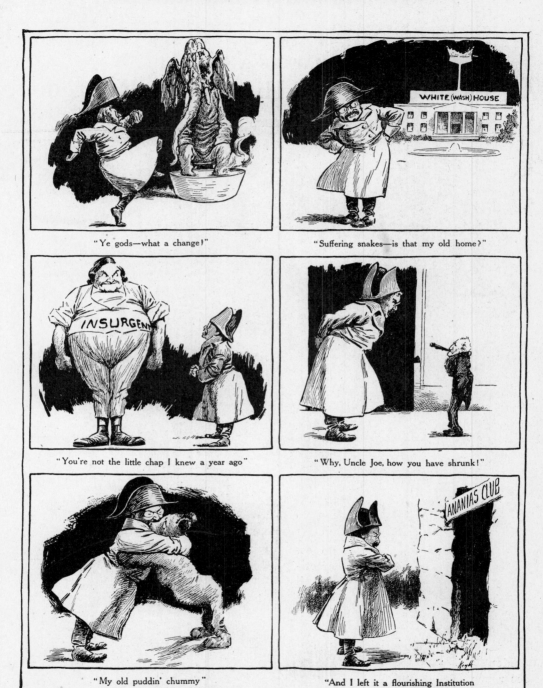

THEODORE IN WONDERLAND (A YEAR'S CHANGES)
From *Collier's Weekly* (New York)

An Ex-President in His Active Retirement

IS IT POSSIBLE?

(In response to numerous questions, Mr. Roosevelt announced on returning from abroad that he would have nothing to say on political subjects for two months.)
From the *Press* (Philadelphia)

HIS FORMER MASTER'S VOICE
From the *Pioneer Press* (St. Paul)

are others who would not permit them to hold any kind of public office. John Quincy Adams, after leaving the White House, in 1829, was elected to the House of Represen-

JUST A CASE OF NERVES
From the *Herald* (Washington)

BACK ON THE JOB AGAIN
From the *Traveler* (Boston)

ROOSEVELT (to Uncle Sam): "Come, little boy, and take your medicine."
From *Judge*

PRESIDENT TAFT TO COLONEL ROOSEVELT: " I, too, have not been idle." (Mr. Taft presents his little bills,—Railroad, Statehood, Postal-Savings Banks and Conservation.)

From the *Record-Herald* (Chicago)

than two years after his retirement in 1885. President Hayes retired to his country home in Ohio, in 1881, after four years in the White House, and died in 1893. He was highly useful, for twelve years, in many causes of philanthropy and education.

General Grant was an ex-President for eight years, and most of that period was actively spent in a blaze of publicity. His tour around the world occupied more than two years, from May 17, 1877, to November 12, 1879. He was received with the highest honors in all the countries he visited. In the years immediately following he visited Mexico and Cuba, and was a United States commissioner to make a commercial treaty with Mexico. In 1880 he was again a candidate for the Presidency, his name holding together a large body of delegates through thirty-six

tatives, where he served for eighteen years,—until his death,—as a contentious and eloquent member of Congress.

President Cleveland was sixty years old when he left the White House in 1897, and he died at the age of seventy-one. His quiet and consistent life at Princeton was not without its relation to public opinion and the country's affairs; but his health was not vigorous, and his life as an ex-President was private rather than public.

President Harrison practiced law and wrote an excellent book on constitutional government in the short period of life remaining to him after leaving office in 1893. President Arthur lived less

T. R. HAD A PRIVATE INTERVIEW WITH PRESIDENT TAFT. WHAT WAS THE SUBJECT OF CONVERSATION?

From the *Spokesman-Review* (Spokane)

THE ACCOUNTING
T. R. TO TAFT: "Well, how did this happen? What!"
From the *Sun* (Baltimore)

IF FEET HAD EARS (Mr. Roosevelt visits President
Taft at Beverly)
From the *Ohio State Journal* (Columbus)

ballots. In the period of illness before his death, he wrote his memoirs, without dreaming of the importance of this contribution to our knowledge of the Civil War and of his own career.

Of the earlier ex-Presidents, Jefferson was by far the most influential. He retired from the Presidency in March, 1809, and died July 4, 1826. His seventeen years of retirement were spent, for the most part, at his Virginia home, Monticello; but he was during all that time the real head of the great political party to which he belonged, and his relation to public affairs was constant and important. In this period of retirement, also he founded and created the University of Virginia, and produced much that appears in his collected writings.

ROOSEVELT—"BILLY, I'VE SPIED YOU FIRST."   TAFT—"PEEK-A-BOO, TEDDY."
THERE'S ONLY A LITTLE DIFFERENCE BETWEEN THEM
From the *Meddler* (Cincinnati)

THE SICK REPUBLICAN ELEPHANT: "Dollars to dough-nuts that's Oyster Bay! Wonder if I'll be allowed to land? I'd like to get a few words of comfort from the doctor."

From *Collier's Weekly* (New York)

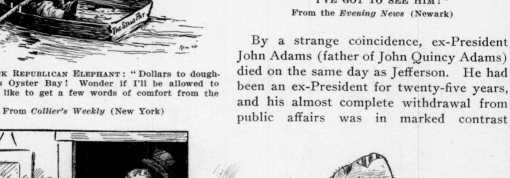

"I'VE GOT TO SEE HIM!"
From the *Evening News* (Newark)

By a strange coincidence, ex-President John Adams (father of John Quincy Adams) died on the same day as Jefferson. He had been an ex-President for twenty-five years, and his almost complete withdrawal from public affairs was in marked contrast

HURRY, DOCTOR!
From the *Eagle* (Brooklyn)

"THINGS HAVEN'T BEEN THE SAME, THEODORE!"
From the *Plain Dealer* (Cleveland)

THE COLONEL AND HIS BOOKS

(Theodore Roosevelt held conferences to-day with State Senator Cobb, Congressman Parsons, and other politicians. After his visitors left Colonel Roosevelt said: " We have had some very interesting talks on literature."—*Dispatch from New York*.)

From the *Sun* (Baltimore)

THE PEACEMAKER

" Gitche Manito, the mighty,
Calls the tribes of men together,
Calls the warriors to his council
By the signal of the peace-pipe."

(Apropos of Colonel Roosevelt's numerous visitors, from all factions of the Republican party.)

From the *Eagle* (Brooklyn)

with Jefferson's varied and vital activities. President Jackson, after his eight years in the White House, imitated Washington

ALL ROADS LEAD TO OYSTER BAY
From the *Journal* (Minneapolis)

THE ANNOUNCEMENT AND ITS EFFECT
Colonel Roosevelt is to make a speech in the Indiana
campaign.—News item from the *Tribune* (South Bend)

in the issuing of a farewell address to the nation, and retired to his home called the Hermitage, near Nashville, Tenn. Like Mr. Roosevelt, he had influence enough to select, nominate, and help elect his successor; and he remained an influential public personage during the remaining eight years of his life.

An exceedingly active and untiring ex-

"WELL, WHAT ARE YOU BOYS HANGING AROUND FOR?"
From the *Leader* (Cleveland)

**"WE'VE BEEN TO OYSTER BAY!
O.K.! O.K.! O.K.!"**
From the *Plain Dealer* (Cleveland)

President was Jackson's successor, Martin Van Buren. He was President from 1837 to 1841,—running for a second term in 1840 but beaten by William Henry Harrison, of the opposing party. Four years later, in 1844, Van Buren was again a candidate before the Democratic convention, where he had a clear majority of the delegates but was unable, on account of the "two-thirds rule," to win the nomination. He had opposed the annexation of Texas, and the Southern Democrats

ANOTHER DARING FLIGHT?
From the *Leader* (Cleveland)

THE JUDGMENT OF A SOLOMON
From the *World-Herald* (Omaha)

nominated and elected James K. Polk against Henry Clay. By 1848, ex-President Van Buren had gone over to the Free Soil movement, and was the Presidential nominee of the new party. His candidacy won no electoral votes, but it defeated the Democrats and put the Whigs into power. He was an active supporter of Pierce in 1852, of Buchanan in 1856, and stood with his party against Lincoln in 1860. But he became a War Democrat, supporting Lincoln's policies until his own death in 1862, at his country home near Kinderhook, New York.

However men may differ as to the public uses to make of an ex-President, most

KEEPING THE OLD ELEPHANT WORRIED
From the *Picayune* (New Orleans)

WHICH WAY?
From the *Record* (Fort Worth)

AS IT WAS   AS IT MAY BE
From the *Spokesman Review* (Spokane)

men of thought and experience would agree that there ought to be some salary or pension granted him,—as to a retired judge,—until his death. Mr. Monroe and General Grant were not the only ex-Presidents whose last days were more or less clouded by financial difficulties. Mr. Roosevelt, returning to the plaudits and greetings of a friendly nation, was subject to extraordinary expenditures by reason of those numerous demands of hospitality, correspondence, travel, and the like, that a public man cannot evade.

Mr. Roosevelt had agreed, before going abroad, to make use of a room in the editorial offices of the *Outlook,* a weekly family paper published in New York, and to contribute to the paper as he might be able. He had also to put his new book through the press, and to prepare the speeches which he had agreed to make at the John Brown celebration in Kansas, the Conservation Congress at St. Paul, and on other occasions, at the end of August and in the months of September and October.

RESTING
From the *Traveler* (Boston)

THE STRENUOUS CONTRIBUTOR
From the *Inter-Ocean* (Chicago)

HON. ANANIAS N SURGENT CAME DOWN THE HILL YESTERDAY. HE WAS ALL SMILES. "I CANNOT SAY WHAT PASSED BETWEEN ME AND THE COL. BUT I AM WILLING TO ADMIT, IF HARD PRESSED, THAT THE COL. HAS PROMISED ME HIS SUPPORT," SAID THE HON ANANIAS.

SEN. MOSSBACK, OF THE OLD GUARD, CAME DOWN SAGAMORE HILL YESTERDAY SMILING BROADLY. HE REFUSED TO TALK FOR PUBLICATION AND TOLD A REPORTER THAT THE COL. HAD PROMISED HIM HIS SUPPORT.

REPRESENTATIVE SCADS, THE BOSSES' LAST HOPE, CAME DOWN THE HILL YESTERDAY. HE LOOSENED UP HIS BROAD SMILE LONG ENOUGH TO SAY THAT THE COL. HAD PROMISED HIM HIS SUPPORT.

SPECIAL THE RIGHT PICTURES WILL NOT BE SHOWN IN OYSTER BAY.

ARE YOU GLOOMY? VISIT SAGAMORE HILL AND CHEER UP
From the *Press* (New York)

SENATOR BEVERIDGE WILL HAVE A GOOD STARTER
(Colonel Roosevelt is to speak in Indiana)
From the *Pioneer Press* (St. Poul)

He had gone to Harvard College at commencement time, where he had met Governor Hughes of New York and paid his respects to President Taft, who was summering at Beverly, Mass. Meanwhile, except for a few hours a week at the *Outlook* office, he was at home at Sagamore Hill, where many public men from different parts of the country called upon

HUGHES GETS T. R.'S "O. K." WILL HE ALSO LABEL TAFT?
From the *World* (New York)

THE SKY-LINE OF OYSTER BAY WHEN GOVERNOR HUGHES APPEARED
From the *Press* (New York)

THE BRONCO BUSTER
From the *World* (New York)

EATING OUT OF HIS HAND
From the *World* (New York)

him, and where it was believed by the newspapers and the cartoonists that he was much interested in hearing about the political affairs of the State of New York and the strain in the Republican party between the regulars and the so-called "insurgents" or "progressives."

It was known that he would visit Indiana to make a speech on behalf of the re-election of Senator Beveridge, and this was regarded as an indorsement of the "progres-

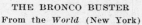

HARD TO TUNE
From the *Evening News* (Newark)

HUNTING A CANDIDATE
From the *Record* (Philadelphia)

INCOGNITO!

(Referring to Colonel Roosevelt's visit to the coal mines of the anthracite region in Pennsylvania in the early part of August)

From the *American* (New York)

SENATOR CUMMINS' NEW PARTY

(Apropos of a proposal attributed to Senator Cummins on account of a statement made in the Des Moines *News*, which is supposed to be the Senator's personal organ)

From the *Inter-Ocean* (Chicago)

sives." It was also known that he would make a speech on behalf of Senator Lodge's re-election in Massachusetts, and this was said to be a matter of personal friendship rather than of championship of the New England junta of high-tariff Senators.

Unquestionably, Mr. Roosevelt's general sympathies were with progressive movements in the Republican party. At the moment when Governor Hughes had called a

A MODERN TOWER OF BABEL
From the *Herald* (New York)

MAKING IMPROVEMENTS!
From the *Eagle* (Brooklyn, N. Y.)

LIONIZATION—SPECULATION—PERTURBATION.—From *Harper's Weekly* (New York)

THE LION: "I wish I knew what you are going to do with me."
T. R. (thoughtfully): "So do I." CHORUS FROM WINDOW: "So do we."

WHAT TO DO WITH THE BOY
From the *Leader* (Cleveland)

"RETIRE ME! WHY, I'VE JUST BEGUN!
I'M ONLY 50."
From the *Record-Herald* (Chicago)

special session of the New York Legislature, Mr. Roosevelt at the Governor's request had declared himself in favor of the Governor's bill for primary elections. In the preliminary plans for the New York

State convention, and in the discussion of possible candidates for the Governorship, Mr. Roosevelt's influence was undoubtedly against the further control of the so-called "machine" or "Old Guard," and in favor of Republican progress as it had been exemplified by men of the type of Governor Hughes.

PRESIDENT TAFT, TO MR. ROOSEVELT: "Quit your crowding."
From the *Sun* (Baltimore)

And it was well known in advance that this spirit would be expressed in the speech to be delivered at Ossawatomie, Kansas, on the last day of August. It had become evident that Mr. Roosevelt was to be highly active, and to regard the ex-Presidency as a post of public duty. It was also clear that the cartoonists would find it necessary to keep him under continued observation, and that a record like this which had been prepared with some historical perspective must needs end abruptly, or else be continued in daily postscripts.

"BOY! THERE'S NOTHING LIKE HIM IN HISTORY"
From the *Pioneer Press* (St. Paul)

From the *World* (New York)